A Traveler's Guide to the Camino Adventure

"Everything You Need to Know for a Successful Pilgrimage"

Lorraine Alvis

Table of Contents

Introduction

Chapter 1:Introduction to the Camino de Santiago

History and Significance
The Routes Explained
Reasons to Walk the Camino
Planning Your Pilgrimage

Chapter 2: Preparing for the Journey

Physical Preparation and Training
Essential Gear and Packing List
Understanding Pilgrim Credentials and Passports
Health and Safety Tips

Chapter 3: The Camino Francés

Overview of the Route
Key Starting Points and Stages
Must-See Landmarks and Destinations
Insider Tips for Accommodation and Dining

Chapter 4: The Camino Portugués

Overview of the Route
Key Starting Points and Stages
Highlights and Points of Interest
Insider Tips for a Smooth Journey

Chapter 5: The Camino del Norte:

Overview of the Route
Coastal Beauty and Challenges
Important Stops and Cultural Insights
Accommodation and Dining
Recommendations

Chapter 6: Lesser-Known Routes

The Via de la Plata
The Camino Primitivo

Chapter 10: Insider Tips and Resources

**Stories and Insights from Experienced
Pilgrims
Recommended Films and documentaries
Useful Apps and Websites
Staying Connected with the Camino
Community**

Introduction

Welcome to Camino de Santiago, a journey that has captivated the hearts and minds of pilgrims for centuries. Whether you are embarking on this adventure for spiritual growth, personal discovery, or the challenge of a lifetime, this guide is designed to be your trusted companion every step of the way.

The Camino de Santiago, or the Way of Saint James, is not just a single path but a network of routes leading to the cathedral of Santiago de Compostela in Galicia, Spain, where the remains of the apostle Saint James are believed to be buried. Each year, thousands of pilgrims from all corners of the globe walk these routes, each bringing their own unique stories and reasons for undertaking the pilgrimage.

This guide offers comprehensive insights into the Camino's most popular routes, including the Camino Francés, the Camino Portugués, and the Camino del Norte. We'll provide you with essential information on planning, preparation, and what to expect on your journey. From physical training tips and packing essentials to navigating the diverse accommodations and understanding the cultural significance of the Camino, we've got you covered.

Beyond the logistical aspects, this guide aims to immerse you in the rich tapestry of experiences that make the Camino de Santiago so special. You'll explore the history, art, and architecture of the regions you pass through, savor local culinary delights, and engage with fellow pilgrims, each contributing to the vibrant community spirit of the Camino.

You'll also find stories and advice from experienced pilgrims who have walked the paths before you. Their insights will inspire and guide you, offering practical tips and heartfelt reflections to enrich your own journey.

Whether you are a seasoned hiker or a first-time pilgrim, this guide will equip you with the knowledge and confidence to embark on your Camino de Santiago. Prepare to be challenged, inspired, and transformed as you walk through picturesque landscapes, historic towns, and spiritual milestones.

So, lace up your boots, grab your pilgrim's passport, and step onto the path that has welcomed so many before you. Your Camino de Santiago adventure awaits, and this guide is here to ensure you make the most of every moment. Welcome to the beginning of an extraordinary journey.

Chapter 1

Introduction to the Camino de Santiago

History and Significance

The Camino de Santiago, also known as the Way of Saint James, has a rich history that spans over a thousand years. This pilgrimage route culminates at the cathedral of Santiago de Compostela in northwestern Spain, where the remains of Saint James the Great, one of Jesus Christ's apostles, are believed to be interred.

The origins of the Camino date back to the 9th century when the tomb of Saint James was discovered in Galicia. According to legend, his remains were miraculously transported from Jerusalem to Spain. This discovery transformed the small town of Santiago de Compostela into one of the most important pilgrimage destinations in Christendom, alongside Rome and Jerusalem.

During the Middle Ages, the Camino de Santiago became a major religious pilgrimage route, attracting thousands of pilgrims from all over Europe. These early pilgrims, known as peregrinos, walked for months, enduring great hardships and dangers, driven by faith and the promise of indulgences granted by the church.

The routes they followed traversed diverse landscapes, passing through bustling towns and serene countryside, each step imbued with spiritual significance.

The pilgrimage experienced a decline during the Reformation and the subsequent Enlightenment period, but it never completely disappeared. The 20th century saw a revival of interest in the Camino, fueled by a renewed sense of spiritual seeking and the promotion of the route by various cultural and religious organizations. Today, the Camino de Santiago attracts a diverse mix of pilgrims—religious devotees, adventure seekers, and those simply looking for a unique experience.

The Camino de Santiago is not just a single path but a network of routes that spread across Europe, each offering its own unique journey. The most popular route is the Camino Francés, starting from Saint-Jean-Pied-de-Port in France and stretching approximately 800 kilometers to Santiago de Compostela. Other notable routes include the Camino Portugués, beginning in Lisbon or Porto, and the Camino del Norte, which follows the northern coast of Spain.

Walking the Camino de Santiago is a transformative experience for many. Pilgrims often speak of the profound sense of community they encounter, the simplicity of life on the road, and the time for introspection and personal growth. The journey is as much about the inner path as it is about the physical trek, with many pilgrims finding new perspectives and a deeper sense of purpose.

The Camino de Santiago holds cultural and historical significance beyond its religious roots. It is a living museum of medieval art and architecture, with countless churches, cathedrals, and monuments dotting the landscape. UNESCO has recognized several Camino routes as World Heritage Sites, acknowledging their importance in the cultural heritage of Europe.

In essence, the Camino de Santiago is a journey of discovery—of landscapes, cultures, history, and oneself. Whether you walk for faith, reflection, or adventure, the Camino offers an experience unlike any other, steeped in centuries of tradition and human spirit. As you embark on your own Camino, you join a long lineage of pilgrims whose footsteps have shaped this enduring path.

The Routes Explained

The Camino de Santiago is not just a single path but a collection of routes that traverse various regions of Europe, each converging at the shrine of Saint James in Santiago de Compostela. While the Camino Francés is the most famous and frequently traveled, there are several other routes, each with its own unique characteristics and appeal. Here, we will explore the main routes and what makes each one special.

1. The Camino Francés

Starting Point: Saint-Jean-Pied-de-Port, France
Distance: Approximately 800 kilometers
Duration: 30-35 days

The Camino Francés is the most popular and well-known route. It begins in the small French town of Saint-Jean-Pied-de-Port, crosses the Pyrenees into Spain, and passes through notable cities such as Pamplona, Logroño, Burgos, and León before reaching Santiago de Compostela. This route is well-marked and offers a variety of accommodations, making it suitable for both novice and experienced pilgrims. The terrain varies from mountainous regions to flat plains, providing a diverse and scenic journey.

2. The Camino Portugués

Starting Point: Lisbon or Porto, Portugal
Distance: Approximately 600 kilometers from Lisbon, 260 kilometers from Porto
Duration: 25-30 days from Lisbon, 10-14 days from Porto

The Camino Portugués is the second most popular route. Pilgrims can start in Lisbon for a longer journey or in Porto for a shorter trek. This route takes you through beautiful Portuguese countryside and historic towns, such as Coimbra and Ponte de Lima, before crossing into Spain at Tui. The Camino Portugués is known for its lush landscapes, charming villages, and a generally milder climate compared to the Camino Francés.

3. The Camino del Norte

Starting Point: Irún, Spain
Distance: Approximately 825 kilometers
Duration: 35-40 days

The Camino del Norte, also known as the Northern Way, follows the northern coast of Spain, offering stunning coastal views and a cooler climate. This route is less crowded than the Camino Francés and is known for its natural beauty and challenging terrain. Pilgrims will pass through cities like San Sebastián, Bilbao, and Santander. The Northern Way offers a blend of coastal scenery, forests, and rolling hills.

4. The Camino Primitivo

Starting Point: Oviedo, Spain
Distance: Approximately 320 kilometers
Duration: 12-15 days

The Camino Primitivo, or Original Way, is considered the oldest route of the Camino de Santiago. It begins in Oviedo and merges with the Camino Francés in Melide. This route is known for its rugged and mountainous terrain, offering a challenging yet rewarding experience. It is less crowded and provides a sense of solitude and connection with nature. The Camino Primitivo is ideal for those seeking a more authentic and off-the-beaten-path pilgrimage.

5. The Via de la Plata

Starting Point: Seville, Spain
Distance: Approximately 1,000 kilometers
Duration: 40-50 days

The Via de la Plata, or Silver Way, is one of the longest Camino routes. It starts in Seville and travels north through the heart of Spain, passing through historic cities such as Mérida, Cáceres, and Salamanca. This route offers a unique blend of Roman history, vast landscapes, and cultural diversity. The Via de la Plata is less frequented, providing a tranquil and reflective journey.

6. The Camino Inglés

Starting Point: Ferrol or A Coruña, Spain
Distance: Approximately 120 kilometers from Ferrol, 75

kilometers from A Coruña
Duration: 5-7 days

The Camino Inglés, or English Way, was historically used by pilgrims from the British Isles. This shorter route begins in the port towns of Ferrol or A Coruña and is ideal for those with limited time. Despite its shorter distance, it offers beautiful coastal and rural scenery, and it is less crowded, making for a peaceful pilgrimage.

7. The Camino Finisterre-Muxía

Starting Point: Santiago de Compostela, Spain
Distance: Approximately 90 kilometers to Finisterre, 120 kilometers to Muxía
Duration: 3-5 days

The Camino Finisterre-Muxía is unique in that it starts in Santiago de Compostela and heads westward to the Atlantic coast. Many pilgrims walk this route as an extension of their pilgrimage to reach "the end of the world" at Cape Finisterre or the beautiful town of Muxía. This route offers stunning coastal landscapes and a profound sense of completion for many pilgrims.

Each route of the Camino de Santiago offers its own distinct experience, challenges, and rewards. Whether you choose the well-trodden Camino Francés or the scenic Camino del Norte, you will find a path that resonates with your personal journey and aspirations. As you walk these historic routes, you join a centuries-old tradition of pilgrimage, connecting with the landscape, the culture, and your fellow pilgrims in a deeply meaningful way.

Reasons to Walk the Camino

The Camino de Santiago attracts pilgrims from all walks of life, each with their own unique motivations and goals. Whether you're seeking spiritual enlightenment, personal growth, or simply an adventurous escape, the Camino offers something for everyone. Here are some of the most compelling reasons to walk the Camino de Santiago:

1. Spiritual and Religious Significance

For many, the Camino de Santiago is a deeply spiritual journey. Pilgrims walk the ancient routes to pay homage to Saint James the Great, seeking a sense of connection to their faith and the long history of the pilgrimage. The journey provides ample time for reflection, prayer, and spiritual renewal, making it a transformative experience for those on a religious quest.

2. Personal Growth and Self-Discovery

Walking the Camino offers an unparalleled opportunity for introspection and personal growth. The simplicity of life on the trail allows for deep contemplation and self-reflection. Many pilgrims find clarity, strength, and a renewed sense of purpose as they face the physical and mental challenges of the journey.

3. Physical Challenge and Adventure

The Camino de Santiago is a physically demanding endeavor that tests endurance and resilience. The varying terrains, from mountainous paths to flat plains, offer a rewarding challenge for outdoor enthusiasts and adventure seekers. Completing the Camino provides a sense of accomplishment and pride in having undertaken and finished such a rigorous journey.

4. Cultural Immersion

The Camino routes pass through diverse regions, each with its own unique culture, history, and traditions. Walking the Camino allows pilgrims to immerse themselves in the local way of life, from sampling regional cuisine to participating in local festivals. The journey is a cultural tapestry woven with the stories and customs of the places you visit.

5. Connection with Nature

The Camino de Santiago offers an opportunity to disconnect from the modern world's hustle and bustle and reconnect with nature. Pilgrims walk through some of Europe's most beautiful landscapes, from lush forests and rolling hills to scenic coastlines and picturesque villages. This close interaction with nature provides a sense of peace and tranquility.

6. Meeting New People and Building Community

One of the most enriching aspects of the Camino is the sense of camaraderie among pilgrims. Walking the Camino fosters deep connections with fellow travelers from around the world, creating a unique and supportive community. The shared experiences, conversations, and friendships formed along the way often become one of the most cherished memories of the pilgrimage.

7. Historical Exploration

The Camino de Santiago is a living museum of medieval history. Pilgrims walk in the footsteps of countless others who have traveled these routes over the centuries. The journey is dotted with historical landmarks, ancient churches, and Roman ruins, offering a fascinating glimpse into Europe's rich past.

8. Mindfulness and Mental Well-being

The repetitive nature of walking, combined with the beauty of the surroundings, encourages a mindful state. Pilgrims often experience a sense of calm and mental clarity, helping to alleviate stress and anxiety. The Camino provides a break from daily routines and the constant bombardment of digital distractions, promoting overall mental well-being.

9. Sense of Achievement

Reaching Santiago de Compostela and standing before the cathedral is a powerful moment of achievement. The physical and emotional effort required to complete the pilgrimage makes this moment profoundly rewarding. Many pilgrims also continue to Finisterre or Muxía to further extend their sense of accomplishment.

10. A Unique Travel Experience

Unlike typical vacations, the Camino de Santiago offers a unique travel experience that combines elements of adventure, spirituality, and cultural exploration. It's a journey where the process is just as important as the destination, providing a deeply enriching and unforgettable experience.

Walking the Camino de Santiago is a multifaceted adventure that touches the mind, body, and soul. Whether you're drawn to it for spiritual reasons, the physical challenge, or the desire for cultural immersion, the Camino offers an experience that can be life-changing. As you prepare to embark on this journey, remember that each step you take is part of a larger tapestry of pilgrimage, woven with the hopes, dreams, and stories of countless pilgrims who have walked before you.

Planning Your Pilgrimage

Embarking on the Camino de Santiago requires thoughtful planning and preparation to ensure a successful and enjoyable journey. From choosing the right route to packing the essential gear, each aspect of preparation is crucial. Here's a comprehensive guide to help you plan your pilgrimage.

1. Choosing Your Route

The first step in planning your pilgrimage is selecting the route that best suits your interests, fitness level, and time availability. Each route offers a unique experience:

Camino Francés: The most popular route, offering a variety of landscapes and well-developed infrastructure.

Camino Portugués: Ideal for those looking for a shorter and less crowded path, with beautiful Portuguese and Spanish countryside.

Camino del Norte: Offers stunning coastal views and a more challenging terrain.

Camino Primitivo: The oldest route, known for its rugged and scenic beauty.

Via de la Plata: A long and diverse route passing through the heart of Spain.

Camino Inglés: A shorter route with coastal and rural scenery.

Camino Finisterre-Muxía: An extension from Santiago to the coast, often walked as a final leg.

2. Deciding When to Go

The timing of your pilgrimage can significantly impact your experience. Consider the following factors:

Weather: The best times to walk the Camino are spring (April to June) and fall (September to October), offering mild temperatures and fewer crowds. Summer (July and August) can be very hot and crowded, while winter (November to March) can be cold and wet, with some accommodations closed.

Festivals: Participating in local festivals can enhance your experience. For example, Santiago's Feast Day on July 25th is a major event.

Personal Schedule: Align your pilgrimage with your personal and work commitments, ensuring you have enough time to complete your chosen route without rushing.

3. Physical Preparation

Walking the Camino de Santiago requires good physical fitness. Begin training several months in advance:

Walking Practice: Gradually increase your walking distance and duration. Aim to walk 15-20 kilometers several times a week, carrying a backpack similar to what you'll use on the Camino.

Strength Training: Incorporate exercises to strengthen your legs, core, and back to support the physical demands of long-distance walking.

Hiking Terrain: If possible, practice on varied terrains, including hills and uneven paths, to simulate the conditions of the Camino.

4. Packing Essentials

Packing light is crucial for a comfortable pilgrimage. Here's a list of essential items:

Backpack: A comfortable, well-fitting backpack with a capacity of 30-40 liters.

Footwear: Sturdy, well-broken-in hiking boots or shoes and a pair of lightweight sandals for evening wear.

Clothing: Moisture-wicking, quick-dry clothes, including layers for varying temperatures. Pack minimally but ensure you have enough to stay comfortable.

Rain Gear: A good quality rain jacket and backpack cover.

Sleeping Gear: Lightweight sleeping bag or liner, suitable for the season.

Personal Items: Toiletries, first aid kit, blister care supplies, sunscreen, hat, and sunglasses.

Pilgrim Passport (Credential): Essential for staying in pilgrim accommodations and collecting stamps along the way.

Guidebook and Maps: A reliable guidebook for your chosen route and any necessary maps or apps.

5. Budgeting

Planning a budget ensures you can manage expenses without stress. Consider the following:

Accommodation: Costs vary depending on the type of lodging, from free or donation-based albergues to private hostels and hotels.

Food: Budget for daily meals, including the pilgrim menu, which offers affordable set meals.

Miscellaneous: Allow for transportation costs, such as flights, trains, or buses to and from your starting and ending points, as well as occasional splurges on treats or souvenirs.

6. Travel Logistics

Plan your travel to and from the Camino:

Starting Point: Determine the best way to reach your starting point, whether by plane, train, bus, or a combination. Major starting points like Saint-Jean-Pied-de-Port, Porto, and Seville are well-connected.

Returning Home: Plan your return journey from Santiago de Compostela or your final destination, considering the most convenient and cost-effective options.

7. Accommodations

Research the types of accommodations available along your route:

Albergues: Pilgrim hostels that offer basic, affordable lodging. Some require reservations, especially during peak seasons.

Private Hostels and Hotels: More comfortable options, often with private rooms and additional amenities. Book in advance during busy periods.

8. Navigating the Camino

While the Camino is well-marked, it's helpful to have resources for navigation:

Guidebooks: A good guidebook provides detailed maps, route descriptions, and information on accommodations and services.

Apps: Download Camino-specific apps for maps, route planning, and real-time information on accommodations and amenities.

9. Health and Safety

Prioritize your health and safety:

Medical Check-Up: Consult your doctor before embarking on the pilgrimage, especially if you have any health concerns.

Insurance: Obtain travel insurance that covers medical emergencies, trip cancellations, and lost or stolen belongings.

Safety Tips: Stay aware of your surroundings, keep valuables secure, and follow local guidelines and advice.

10. Mental and Emotional Preparation

Prepare yourself mentally and emotionally for the journey:

Set Intentions: Reflect on why you are undertaking the pilgrimage and what you hope to gain from the experience.

Stay Open-Minded: Be open to the unexpected, embrace the challenges, and appreciate the journey as much as the destination.

By thoroughly planning your pilgrimage, you can ensure a smoother, more enjoyable experience on the Camino de Santiago. Embrace the preparation process as the first step of your journey, setting the stage for a memorable and transformative adventure.

Chapter 2

Preparing for the Journey

Physical Preparation and Training

Walking the Camino de Santiago is a physically demanding adventure that requires adequate preparation to ensure you can handle the journey comfortably and safely. Here are essential steps and tips to help you prepare physically and train effectively for the Camino.

1. Start Training Early

Begin your training regimen at least three to six months before your planned departure date. This time frame allows your body to adapt gradually to the physical demands of long-distance walking and minimizes the risk of injury.

2. Walking Practice

The foundation of your training should be regular walking. Follow these guidelines to build your endurance:

Gradual Increase: Start with shorter walks and gradually increase the distance and duration. Aim to walk at least three to four times a week.

Long Walks: Incorporate longer walks on weekends, gradually building up to distances of 15-20 kilometers (9-12 miles). These longer sessions will simulate a typical day on the Camino.

Backpack Practice: Train with a loaded backpack similar to what you'll carry on the Camino. Start with a lighter load and gradually increase the weight to get used to carrying it for extended periods.

3. Strength Training

Incorporate strength training exercises to build the muscles you'll rely on during your pilgrimage. Focus on the following areas:

Legs: Squats, lunges, and step-ups help strengthen your quadriceps, hamstrings, and calves.

Core: Planks, crunches, and Russian twists improve core stability, essential for balance and posture.

Back: Exercises like deadlifts and rows strengthen your back muscles, which support your backpack and overall posture.

4. Flexibility and Mobility

Maintaining flexibility and mobility is crucial for preventing injuries and ensuring comfort:

Stretching: Incorporate a regular stretching routine to improve flexibility in your legs, hips, and back. Focus on hamstrings, calves, hip flexors, and lower back.

Yoga: Practicing yoga can enhance flexibility, balance, and mental focus. Consider adding a yoga session to your weekly routine.

5. Hiking Terrain

Simulate the conditions you'll encounter on the Camino by training on varied terrains:

Hills: Include uphill and downhill walks to prepare for the elevation changes you'll face on the Camino.

Uneven Surfaces: Walk on trails, gravel paths, and rocky terrain to strengthen your ankles and improve balance.

Stairs: Climbing stairs can mimic the effort of walking uphill and help build leg strength.

6. Foot Care

Healthy feet are vital for a successful pilgrimage. Follow these tips to take care of your feet during training and on the Camino:

Footwear: Invest in high-quality, comfortable hiking boots or shoes. Ensure they are well-broken-in before starting the Camino to prevent blisters.

Socks: Wear moisture-wicking, cushioned socks to reduce friction and prevent blisters. Consider using liner socks for added protection.

Foot Care Routine: Keep your feet clean and dry. Use blister prevention methods such as applying lubricants or using blister pads on hot spots.

7. Nutrition and Hydration

Proper nutrition and hydration support your training and overall health:

Balanced Diet: Eat a balanced diet rich in carbohydrates, proteins, and healthy fats to fuel your body and aid in muscle recovery.

Hydration: Stay hydrated by drinking plenty of water throughout the day. During long walks, carry water and consider using electrolyte supplements to replace lost minerals.

8. Listening to Your Body

Pay attention to your body's signals to avoid overtraining and injury:

Rest Days: Incorporate rest days into your training schedule to allow your body to recover and prevent burnout.

Injury Prevention: If you experience pain or discomfort, address it promptly. Seek professional advice if needed and adjust your training as necessary.

9. Mental Preparation

Physical training is important, but mental preparation is equally crucial:

Set Goals: Define your personal goals and motivations for walking the Camino. This mental focus can help you stay motivated during challenging moments.

Visualize Success: Imagine yourself successfully completing the Camino, enjoying the landscapes, and meeting fellow pilgrims. Positive visualization can boost your confidence and mental resilience.

10. Pre-Departure Check-Up

Schedule a check-up with your healthcare provider before you leave:

Medical Clearance: Ensure you are in good health and discuss any pre-existing conditions that may affect your pilgrimage.

Vaccinations: Verify that you have all necessary vaccinations for travel to Spain and any other countries you may pass through.

By following these physical preparation and training guidelines, you'll be well-equipped to handle the demands of the Camino de Santiago. Your journey will be more enjoyable, and you'll reduce the risk of injury, allowing you to fully immerse yourself in the experience. Remember, the effort you put into preparing now will pay off immensely when you set foot on the path to Santiago de Compostela.

Essential Gear and Packing List

Packing the right gear is crucial for a comfortable and successful pilgrimage on the Camino de Santiago. Your goal is to carry only what is necessary to keep your backpack light, yet ensure you have everything you need for the journey. Here's a comprehensive list of essential items to pack:

1. Backpack

Size: 30-40 liters is ideal for most pilgrims.

Features: Look for a backpack with a comfortable fit, good back support, padded shoulder straps, and a waist belt. Ensure it has rain cover or is waterproof.

Fit: Adjust the straps so the weight is distributed evenly across your back and hips.

2. Footwear

Hiking Boots/Shoes: Choose well-broken-in, sturdy hiking boots or trail shoes. Comfort and support are key.

Sandals/Flip-Flops: Lightweight footwear for evenings and showers.

Socks: Moisture-wicking, cushioned socks. Consider packing 3-4 pairs, including liner socks to prevent blisters.

3. Clothing

Base Layers: Moisture-wicking shirts (short and long-sleeved). Pack 2-3 of each.

Trousers/Shorts: Lightweight, quick-dry hiking pants and shorts. Convertible pants are a good option.

Fleece Jacket: For warmth during cooler mornings and evenings.

Rain Gear: A high-quality rain jacket and rain pants or poncho. A backpack cover is also essential.

Underwear: Quick-dry, moisture-wicking underwear. Pack 3-4 pairs.

Hat/Cap: For sun protection.

Buff/Scarf: Multipurpose use for warmth, sun protection, and dust.

4. Sleeping Gear

Sleeping Bag/Liner: Lightweight and appropriate for the season. A sleeping bag liner can be sufficient in warmer months.

Ear Plugs: To ensure a good night's sleep in shared accommodations.

5. Personal Care

Toiletries: Travel-sized items such as toothpaste, toothbrush, soap, shampoo, deodorant, and a quick-dry towel.

First Aid Kit: Basic supplies including band-aids, blister treatment, pain relievers, antiseptic wipes, and any personal medications.

Sunscreen: High SPF to protect against sun exposure.

Lip Balm: With SPF to prevent chapped lips.

Toilet Paper/Wet Wipes: For hygiene in places where facilities may be limited.

6. Navigation and Documentation

Pilgrim Passport (Credential): Essential for staying in pilgrim accommodations and collecting stamps.

Guidebook/Maps: Reliable guidebook for your chosen route and maps if necessary.

Identification: Passport, ID card, and photocopies of important documents.

Money: Cash (euros), credit/debit cards, and a small, secure wallet or money belt.

7. Electronics

Phone/Tablet: For communication, navigation, and entertainment.

Chargers and Adapters: Ensure you have the appropriate plugs for Spain and other countries you may visit.

Headlamp/Flashlight: Useful for early morning starts and staying in dormitories.

8. Miscellaneous

Water Bottle/Hydration System: At least 1 liter capacity. Hydration bladders can be convenient.

Trekking Poles: Helpful for balance and reducing strain on joints.

Laundry Supplies: Small amount of detergent, a travel clothesline, and safety pins for drying clothes.

Reusable Bags: For organizing gear, dirty laundry, and groceries.

Notebook and Pen: To document your journey and reflections.

Small Knife/Multi-tool: Handy for various tasks.

9. Optional Items

Camera: For capturing memories if you prefer not to use your phone.

Small Daypack: For short excursions and to use as a carry-on during travel.

Lightweight Blanket: For extra warmth or comfort.

Binoculars: For bird watching and enjoying distant views.

Tips for Packing

Weight Limit: Aim to keep your backpack's weight below 10% of your body weight. Typically, this means around 6-8 kg (13-17 lbs), excluding water and food.

Packing Order: Place heavier items closer to your back and towards the middle of the pack. Keep frequently used items accessible.

Test Pack: Pack your gear and go on practice walks to ensure everything fits comfortably and you can manage the weight.

By carefully selecting and packing your gear, you can ensure a more comfortable and enjoyable pilgrimage on the Camino de Santiago. Remember, every gram counts, so prioritize multi-use items and pack only what you truly need. With the right preparation, you'll be well-equipped to face the challenges and embrace the joys of this incredible journey.

Understanding Pilgrim Credentials and Passports

The pilgrim passport, known as the "Credencial del Peregrino," is an essential document for anyone walking the Camino de Santiago. It serves multiple purposes, including proving your status as a pilgrim, gaining access to special accommodations, and collecting stamps along your journey. Here's everything you need to know about pilgrim credentials and passports.

What is the Pilgrim Passport?

The pilgrim passport is a small booklet that identifies you as a pilgrim walking the Camino de Santiago. It includes your personal information and spaces for stamps (sellos) from various points along the route. These stamps serve as evidence of your journey and are required to receive the Compostela, a certificate of completion, upon reaching Santiago de Compostela.

Where to Obtain a Pilgrim Passport

You can obtain a pilgrim passport from various places, including:

Pilgrim Offices: Major starting points such as Saint-Jean-Pied-de-Port, Roncesvalles, and Sarria have pilgrim offices where you can get your passport.

Cathedrals and Churches: Many cathedrals and churches along the Camino provide pilgrim passports.

Confraternities of Saint James: These organizations, often found in your home country, can issue passports before you depart.

Online: Some organizations allow you to order a pilgrim passport online and have it mailed to you.

How to Use Your Pilgrim Passport

Using your pilgrim passport is straightforward:

Stamps: Collect stamps from albergues (pilgrim hostels), churches, tourist offices, bars, restaurants, and other establishments along the Camino. Stamps are typically placed in your passport by the staff at these locations.

Frequency: Aim to collect at least one stamp per day. If starting within 100 kilometers of Santiago, such as from Sarria on the Camino Francés, you should collect two stamps per day to qualify for the Compostela.

Information: Fill out your personal details in the passport, including your name, nationality, and starting point.

Benefits of the Pilgrim Passport

The pilgrim passport offers several benefits:

Access to Albergues: Many pilgrim hostels (albergues) only accommodate individuals with a pilgrim passport. This document grants you access to these affordable and often communal lodging options.

Discounts and Special Services: Some establishments, such as restaurants and museums, offer discounts or special services to pilgrims with a credential.

Proof of Pilgrimage: Collecting stamps in your passport provides a tangible record of your journey, showcasing the places you've visited and the distances you've covered.

Certificate of Completion: To receive the Compostela, the official certificate of pilgrimage, you must present your pilgrim passport with the required stamps at the Pilgrim's Office in Santiago de Compostela.

Receiving the Compostela

Upon completing your pilgrimage, you can obtain the Compostela by presenting your pilgrim passport at the Pilgrim's Office in Santiago de Compostela. Here's what you need to do:

Final Destination: Reach the cathedral of Santiago de Compostela, the traditional end point of the Camino.

Pilgrim's Office: Visit the Pilgrim's Office, located near the cathedral. Be prepared for possible lines, especially during peak seasons.

Present Your Passport: Show your pilgrim passport with the collected stamps as proof of your journey. Ensure you have the necessary stamps, especially from the last 100 kilometers (200 kilometers if biking).

Certificate Issuance: The staff will verify your passport and issue the Compostela. You may also receive a distance certificate, which indicates the distance you've traveled.

Tips for Managing Your Pilgrim Passport

Keep It Safe: Protect your pilgrim passport from damage by storing it in a plastic sleeve or a waterproof pouch. Keep it in a secure place in your backpack.

Stamps as Souvenirs: Consider collecting extra stamps beyond the required number. They make excellent keepsakes and memories of your journey.

Backup Plan: If you lose your pilgrim passport, you can usually obtain a replacement from a pilgrim office, though you may need to retrace some steps to recollect necessary stamps.

The pilgrim passport is more than just a piece of paper; it's a symbol of your journey and a key to unlocking the full experience of the Camino de Santiago. By understanding its importance and how to use it, you'll be well-prepared to navigate the route, access essential services, and ultimately receive the Compostela as a testament to your pilgrimage.

Health and Safety Tips

Ensuring your health and safety on the Camino de Santiago is crucial for a successful and enjoyable pilgrimage. The journey can be physically demanding, and taking precautions will help you stay healthy, avoid injuries, and address any emergencies that arise. Here are essential health and safety tips to keep in mind:

1. Pre-Departure Medical Check-Up

Consult Your Doctor: Schedule a medical check-up before your trip to ensure you are in good health and discuss any pre-existing conditions or concerns.

Vaccinations: Ensure your vaccinations are up-to-date. Consult with your doctor about any additional vaccinations that may be recommended for travel to Spain and other regions.

2. Physical Preparation

Training: Engage in regular physical training to build your stamina and strength. Include long walks, strength training, and practice hikes with your backpack to prepare your body for the demands of the Camino.

Stretching: Incorporate a routine of stretching exercises to maintain flexibility and prevent muscle strain.

3. Foot Care

Proper Footwear: Invest in high-quality, well-broken-in hiking boots or shoes. Ensure they provide good support and comfort.

Socks: Wear moisture-wicking, cushioned socks to reduce friction and prevent blisters. Consider using liner socks for added protection.

Blister Prevention: Apply blister prevention methods such as using lubricants, blister pads, or moleskin on hot spots. Keep your feet clean and dry.

4. Hydration and Nutrition

Stay Hydrated: Drink plenty of water throughout the day, especially during long walks. Carry a water bottle or hydration system and refill it regularly.

Balanced Diet: Eat a balanced diet that includes carbohydrates, proteins, and healthy fats to fuel your body and aid in muscle recovery. Include fruits and vegetables for essential vitamins and minerals.

Snacks: Carry nutritious snacks like nuts, dried fruits, and energy bars to maintain your energy levels between meals.

5. Sun Protection

Sunscreen: Apply a high SPF sunscreen to protect your skin from harmful UV rays. Reapply regularly, especially if you are sweating.

Hat and Sunglasses: Wear a wide-brimmed hat and UV-protection sunglasses to shield your face and eyes from the sun.

6. Managing Fatigue and Rest

Pace Yourself: Walk at a comfortable pace and listen to your body. Take regular breaks to rest and recover.

Rest Days: Plan rest days into your schedule to allow your body to recuperate, especially during longer journeys.

Sleep: Ensure you get enough sleep each night to recharge your body for the next day's walk.

7. First Aid Kit

Essentials: Pack a basic first aid kit including band-aids, antiseptic wipes, pain relievers, blister care supplies, and any personal medications.

Insect Repellent: Carry insect repellent to protect against bites and stings.

8. Dealing with Injuries

Minor Injuries: Treat minor injuries such as blisters, cuts, and bruises promptly to prevent infection and further complications.

Seek Medical Help: If you experience severe pain, persistent discomfort, or symptoms of a serious condition, seek medical attention immediately. Familiarize yourself with the locations of medical facilities along your route.

9. Safety on the Trail

Stay on Marked Paths: Follow the marked routes to avoid getting lost. Use guidebooks, maps, and apps to stay on track.

Travel in Pairs or Groups: Whenever possible, walk with others for added safety and companionship.

Be Aware of Your Surroundings: Stay vigilant and aware of your environment. Avoid isolated areas, especially after dark.

Emergency Contacts: Carry a list of emergency contacts, including local authorities and medical facilities. Know the emergency number for Spain (112).

10. Personal Security

Valuables: Keep your valuables secure and hidden. Use a money belt or hidden pouch for cash, cards, and important documents.

Backpack Security: Never leave your backpack unattended. Use a small lock for extra security.

Identification: Carry a photocopy of your passport and other important documents as a backup.

11. Weather Preparedness

Check Weather Reports: Monitor weather forecasts and prepare for changing conditions.

Layered Clothing: Dress in layers to adjust to varying temperatures. Carry rain gear to stay dry in wet weather.

12. Mental Well-Being

Set Realistic Goals: Set achievable daily goals to avoid overexertion and disappointment.

Stay Positive: Maintain a positive attitude and focus on the journey rather than the destination. Take time to enjoy the scenery and experiences.

By following these health and safety tips, you can minimize risks and ensure a more enjoyable and fulfilling experience on the Camino de Santiago. Remember that preparation and awareness are key to a successful pilgrimage, allowing you to fully embrace the journey and all it has to offer.

Chapter 3

The Camino Francés

Overview of the Route

The Camino Francés, or the French Way, is the most popular and well-known route of the Camino de Santiago. This iconic pilgrimage path begins in Saint-Jean-Pied-de-Port, France, and spans approximately 800 kilometers (500 miles) to the cathedral of Santiago de Compostela in Spain. The Camino Francés offers a diverse and enriching experience, taking pilgrims through a variety of landscapes, historic towns, and cultural landmarks. Here is an in-depth overview of the route:

1. Starting Point: Saint-Jean-Pied-de-Port

Location: A charming town in the French Basque Country, nestled at the foot of the Pyrenees. **Significance**: The traditional starting point for many pilgrims, known for its picturesque streets and historic significance.

Highlights: The town's ancient gate, Porte Saint-Jacques, and the 14th Century Church of Notre-Dame-du-bout-du-pont.

2. Crossing the Pyrenees

Challenge: The first stage involves a strenuous climb over the Pyrenees mountains into Spain, offering breathtaking views and a sense of accomplishment.

Route Options: The Route Napoléon (more scenic and challenging) and the Valcarlos Route (lower altitude and safer in bad weather).

3. Navarra Region

Key Towns: Roncesvalles, Pamplona, Puente la Reina, Estella.

Highlights: The medieval monastery in Roncesvalles, the historic city of Pamplona famous for its Running of the Bulls, the Romanesque bridge in Puente la Reina, and the wine fountain in Irache.

4. La Rioja Region

Key Towns: Logroño, Nájera, Santo Domingo de la Calzada.

Highlights: Logroño's vibrant tapas scene, the historic sites in Nájera, and the legend of the chickens in Santo Domingo de la Calzada's cathedral.

5. Castilla y León Region

Key Towns: Burgos, Frómista, Carrión de los Condes, León, Astorga.

Highlights: The Gothic cathedral in Burgos, the Canal de Castilla in Frómista, the Romanesque churches in Carrión de los Condes, the majestic cathedral and lively atmosphere in León, and the Gaudí-designed Episcopal Palace in Astorga.

6. Meseta

Terrain: Flat, open plains that stretch for about 200 kilometers.

Experience: Known for its long, straight paths and the opportunity for deep reflection and solitude.

Key Villages: Hontanas, Castrojeriz, Sahagún.

7. Galicia Region

Key Towns: O Cebreiro, Sarria, Portomarín, Palas de Rei, Arzúa.

Highlights: The ancient village of O Cebreiro with its Celtic heritage, Sarria as a popular starting point for those walking the final 100 kilometers, the Romanesque church in Portomarín, the medieval bridge in Palas de Rei, and the cheese-producing town of Arzúa.

8. Arrival in Santiago de Compostela

Final Stage: The journey culminates in Santiago de Compostela, a city steeped in history and religious significance.

Cathedral: The iconic cathedral where the remains of Saint James are believed to be buried. Pilgrims often attend the Pilgrim's Mass and witness the famous Botafumeiro (giant incense burner) in action.

9. Additional Considerations

Accommodation: A mix of albergues (pilgrim hostels), private hostels, hotels, and guesthouses. Reservations are recommended during peak seasons.

Weather: Varies significantly along the route. Prepare for the cool, wet climate in Galicia and the hot, dry conditions of the Meseta.

Cultural Experiences: Opportunities to engage with local traditions, festivals, and culinary delights throughout the journey.

The Camino Francés offers a rich tapestry of experiences, from the physical challenge of crossing the Pyrenees to the spiritual reward of arriving at the cathedral of Santiago de Compostela. This route is well-marked and supported by a robust network of accommodations and services, making it accessible to pilgrims of all experience levels. Whether you seek spiritual fulfillment, personal growth, or the adventure of a lifetime, the Camino Francés provides a path that is both challenging and deeply rewarding.

Key Starting Points and Stages

The Camino Francés is typically divided into stages, with each stage representing a day's walk. Here are the key starting points and stages along the route:

1. Saint-Jean-Pied-de-Port to Roncesvalles (25 km)

Highlights: The challenging ascent over the Pyrenees, breathtaking mountain views, and the welcoming monastery at Roncesvalles.

2. Roncesvalles to Zubiri (22 km)

Highlights: Descending through lush forests, crossing medieval bridges, and the serene village of Zubiri.

3. Zubiri to Pamplona (21 km)

Highlights: Walking through picturesque countryside, reaching the historic city of Pamplona with its vibrant culture and landmarks.

4. Pamplona to Puente la Reina (24 km)

Highlights: The Alto del Perdón with its pilgrim sculptures, the medieval bridge in Puente la Reina.

5. Puente la Reina to Estella (22 km)

Highlights: Vineyards, olive groves, and the ancient town of Estella.

6. Estella to Los Arcos (21 km)

Highlights: The wine fountain at Irache, scenic rural landscapes.

7. Los Arcos to Logroño (28 km)

Highlights: Entering the La Rioja wine region, exploring Logroño's famous tapas street, Calle Laurel.

8. Logroño to Nájera (30 km)

Highlights: Vineyards, the historic town of Nájera.

9. Nájera to Santo Domingo de la Calzada (21 km)

Highlights: The town of Santo Domingo de la Calzada with its cathedral and pilgrim traditions.

10. Santo Domingo de la Calzada to Belorado (23 km)

Highlights: Rolling hills and quiet villages.

11. Belorado to Burgos (50 km, typically split into two stages)

Highlights: The Gothic cathedral in Burgos, the historic city center.

12. Burgos to Hontanas (31 km)

Highlights: Entering the Meseta, serene and expansive landscapes.

13. Hontanas to Frómista (34 km)

Highlights: The ruins of the Convento de San Antón, the Canal de Castilla.

14. Frómista to Carrión de los Condes (19 km)

Highlights: Romanesque churches and historic sites in Carrión de los Condes.

15. Carrión de los Condes to Sahagún (38 km, typically split into two stages)

Highlights: Peaceful paths through the Meseta, the historic town of Sahagún.

16. Sahagún to León (55 km, typically split into two stages)

Highlights: The lively city of León with its stunning cathedral and vibrant atmosphere.

17. León to Astorga (50 km, typically split into two stages)

Highlights: The Gaudí-designed Episcopal Palace, the historic town of Astorga.

18. Astorga to Rabanal del Camino (21 km)

Highlights: Beginning the ascent into the mountains, the village of Rabanal del Camino.

19. Rabanal del Camino to Ponferrada (32 km)

Highlights: The Cruz de Ferro (Iron Cross), the Templar castle in Ponferrada.

20. Ponferrada to Villafranca del Bierzo (23 km)

Highlights: The vineyards of the Bierzo region, the historic town of Villafranca del Bierzo.

21. Villafranca del Bierzo to O Cebreiro (28 km)

Highlights: The challenging climb to the mountain village of O Cebreiro, known for its Celtic heritage.

22. O Cebreiro to Sarria (40 km, typically split into two stages)

Highlights: Beautiful mountain scenery, the town of Sarria, a common starting point for the final 100 kilometers.

23. Sarria to Portomarín (22 km)

Highlights: Crossing the medieval bridge into Portomarín, known for its Romanesque church.

24. Portomarín to Palas de Rei (25 km)

Highlights: Rolling hills and scenic paths, the town of Palas de Rei.

25. Palas de Rei to Arzúa (29 km)

Highlights: Peaceful woodlands and the cheese-producing town of Arzúa.

26. Arzúa to O Pedrouzo (19 km)

Highlights: Quiet rural landscapes, the village of O Pedrouzo.

27. O Pedrouzo to Santiago de Compostela (20 km)

Highlights: The final stretch to Santiago de Compostela, the emotional arrival at the cathedral, attending the Pilgrim's Mass.

This structured approach to the Camino Francés helps pilgrims manage their journey, providing a sense of progress and accomplishment as they move from one stage to the next. Each stage offers its own unique experiences and challenges, making the pilgrimage a richly varied and deeply rewarding adventure.

Must-See Landmarks and Destinations

The Camino Francés is dotted with numerous landmarks and destinations that offer historical, cultural, and spiritual significance. Here are some must-see landmarks and destinations along the route:

1. Saint-Jean-Pied-de-Port

Porte Saint-Jacques: The ancient gate through which pilgrims pass as they begin their journey.

Church of Notre-Dame-du-Bout-du-Pont: A 14th-century church that marks the traditional starting point.

2. Roncesvalles

Collegiate Church of Roncesvalles: A beautiful Gothic church and monastery providing refuge for pilgrims.

Monastery and Museum: Offers insights into the history of the pilgrimage.

3. Pamplona

Plaza del Castillo: The vibrant main square, perfect for resting and people-watching.

Cathedral of Santa María la Real: A stunning Gothic cathedral with a rich history.

City Walls: Explore the ancient fortifications and get a panoramic view of the city.

4. Puente la Reina

Medieval Bridge: The Romanesque bridge built in the 11th century is a picturesque landmark.

Church of the Crucifix: Known for its unique crucifix and beautiful architecture.

5. Estella

Palace of the Kings of Navarre: A well-preserved Romanesque palace.

Church of San Pedro de la Rúa: A church with impressive Gothic architecture.

Wine Fountain at Irache: Offers free wine for pilgrims, a unique and memorable stop.

6. Logroño

Calle Laurel: Famous for its tapas bars and vibrant nightlife.

Concatedral de Santa María de la Redonda: A beautiful Baroque cathedral.

7. Santo Domingo de la Calzada

Cathedral of Santo Domingo: Known for the legend of the miracle chickens and its impressive architecture.

Medieval Streets: Walk through the historic streets and enjoy the local atmosphere.

8. Burgos

Burgos Cathedral: A UNESCO World Heritage Site, this Gothic cathedral is one of Spain's most magnificent.

Monastery of Las Huelgas: A historical monastery with significant historical artifacts.

9. Frómista

Church of San Martín: An excellent example of Romanesque architecture, dating back to the 11th century.

Canal de Castilla: A scenic and historical canal with beautiful walking paths.

10. León

Cathedral of León: Known for its stunning stained glass windows and Gothic architecture.

Basilica of San Isidoro: Houses the Royal Pantheon, known as the Sistine Chapel of Romanesque art.

Casa Botines: A modernist building designed by Gaudí.

11. Astorga

Episcopal Palace: Another Gaudí masterpiece, this neo-Gothic palace is now a museum.

Astorga Cathedral: A blend of Gothic, Renaissance, and Baroque styles.

12. Ponferrada

Templar Castle: A well-preserved castle built by the Knights Templar, offering great views and historical exhibits.

Basilica de la Encina: Known for its beautiful Renaissance architecture.

13. O Cebreiro

Church of Santa María la Real: An ancient pre-Romanesque church with significant religious artifacts.

Pallozas: Traditional round stone houses that offer a glimpse into the past.

14. Samos

Monastery of Samos: One of the oldest and most significant monasteries in Spain, set in a beautiful valley.

15. Sarria

Church of Santa Mariña: A beautiful Romanesque church.

River Walks: Scenic paths along the river, providing peaceful walking areas.

16. Portomarín

Church of San Nicolás: A Romanesque church moved stone by stone from its original location.

Medieval Bridge: Offers picturesque views of the Miño River.

17. Palas de Rei

Church of San Tirso: A charming church with historical significance.

Castro de Castromaior: Ancient Celtic ruins near the town.

18. Arzúa

Cheese Festival: Known for its delicious local cheese, the town hosts a popular cheese festival.

Church of Santiago: A beautiful church in the heart of Arzúa.

19. Monte do Gozo

Hill of Joy: Offers the first view of the spires of Santiago de Compostela, marking the final approach to the city.

Monument to Pilgrims: Commemorates the millions of pilgrims who have walked the Camino.

20. Santiago de Compostela

Cathedral of Santiago de Compostela: The final destination for pilgrims, housing the remains of Saint

James. The Pilgrim's Mass, often featuring the Botafumeiro, is a must-see.

Plaza del Obradoiro: The main square in front of the cathedral, where pilgrims gather to celebrate their arrival.

Museum of Pilgrimage: Offers insights into the history and significance of the Camino.

These landmarks and destinations add depth and richness to the Camino Francés, making it a journey filled with cultural, historical, and spiritual discoveries. Each stop along the way offers unique experiences and memories, contributing to the overall tapestry of your pilgrimage.

Insider Tips for Accommodation and Dining

The Camino Francés is well-equipped with a range of accommodation and dining options to suit every budget and preference. Here are some insider tips to help you make the most of your experience:

Accommodation Tips

1. Types of Accommodation

Albergues: These are the most common and affordable options for pilgrims. They can be municipal (run by local governments) or private.

Municipal Albergues: Generally cheaper, sometimes donation-based, and operate on a first-come, first-served basis.

Private Albergues: Slightly more expensive but often offer more amenities, such as better bedding, private rooms, or included meals.

Hotels and Hostels: For more comfort, there are plenty of hotels and hostels along the route. These are more expensive but offer privacy and additional services.

Casa Rurales: Country homes converted into guesthouses, offering a unique and comfortable stay often with local charm and home-cooked meals.

Paradors: Luxury state-run hotels located in historic buildings such as castles and monasteries, perfect for a splurge night.

2. Booking and Reservations

Peak Season: During peak seasons (spring and autumn), it's wise to book your accommodation in advance, especially in popular towns.

Off-Peak Season: During off-peak times, you can often find accommodation without booking ahead, giving you more flexibility.

Online Platforms: Use websites and apps like Booking.com, Gronze.com, and Albergues Camino Santiago for reservations and reviews.

Calling Ahead: If you prefer spontaneity, consider calling ahead a day or two to ensure availability.

Pilgrim Pass: Some albergues require a pilgrim credential for access, so always have it on hand.

3. General Tips

Early Arrival: Arrive early in the afternoon to secure a bed in popular albergues, especially in municipal ones.

Rest Days: Plan rest days in larger towns or cities with more accommodation options to ensure you can rest comfortably.

Laundry Facilities: Choose accommodations with laundry facilities to keep your gear fresh. Some albergues offer laundry services or have washing machines and dryers.

Rest and Comfort: Bring earplugs and a sleep mask for shared dormitories to ensure a good night's sleep.

Dining Tips

1. Pilgrim Menus

What to Expect: Most towns and villages offer a "Menú del Peregrino" or Pilgrim's Menu, a three-course meal typically including a starter, main course, dessert, bread, and wine or water.

Cost: Prices range from €10 to €15, making it an affordable and filling option.

Variety: While menus can be repetitive, they offer hearty and local dishes such as lentil soup, paella, roasted chicken, and flan.

2. Local Cuisine

Navarra: Try "chistorra" (spicy sausage) and local pintxos (tapas).

La Rioja: Famous for its wines, enjoy them alongside dishes like "patatas a la riojana" (potatoes with chorizo).

Castilla y León: Known for roast lamb, black pudding (morcilla), and rich stews.

Galicia: Seafood is a highlight, with dishes like "pulpo a la gallega" (Galician octopus) and empanadas. Don't miss the local cheeses and the almond cake, "tarta de Santiago."

3. Breakfast and Snacks

Early Start: Many pilgrims start walking early; grab breakfast in your albergue or a local café. Typical options include coffee, toast, pastries, or tortilla (Spanish omelette).

On the Go: Carry snacks like nuts, dried fruits, energy bars, and fresh fruit to keep your energy up during the day.

Cafés and Bars: Stop at cafés along the route for a mid-morning coffee and a "bocadillo" (sandwich).

4. Hydration

Water: Drink plenty of water throughout the day. Tap water is generally safe, and fountains are available in most towns.

Hydration System: Consider using a hydration bladder for convenience or carry a refillable water bottle.

5. Dining Etiquette

Dining Hours: Spanish meal times are later than in many other countries. Lunch is typically served from 1:30 PM to 3:30 PM, and dinner from 8:00 PM to 10:30 PM.

Sharing Meals: Dining with fellow pilgrims is a great way to build camaraderie. Share tables and enjoy the communal experience.

Tipping: Tipping is not obligatory but appreciated. A small tip for good service is customary.

6. Cooking Your Own Meals

Albergue Kitchens: Some albergues have kitchens where you can cook your own meals. This can be a budget-friendly and social option.

Local Markets: Buy fresh produce and local ingredients from markets and grocery stores to prepare simple, healthy meals.

By following these tips, you can enjoy a comfortable and enriching experience on the Camino Francés. The right accommodation and dining choices will enhance your journey, providing rest and nourishment as you make your way to Santiago de Compostela.

Chapter 4

The Camino Portugués

Overview of the Route

The Camino Portugués, or the Portuguese Way, is the second most popular route of the Camino de Santiago, offering a unique blend of Portuguese and Spanish culture, history, and landscapes. This route begins in Lisbon or Porto, and it covers approximately 600 kilometers (370 miles) from Lisbon or about 260 kilometers (160 miles) from Porto to the cathedral of Santiago de Compostela in Spain. Here is an in-depth overview of the Camino Portugués:

Starting Points

Lisbon: Starting in the vibrant capital of Portugal, the route from Lisbon is approximately 600 kilometers and takes about 25-30 days to complete. This less-traveled path offers a rich cultural and historical experience through central Portugal.

Porto: The more popular starting point, this scenic route begins in Porto, known for its port wine, picturesque Douro River, and stunning architecture. The route from Porto is approximately 260 kilometers and takes about

10-14 days to complete, offering a more manageable distance for many pilgrims.

Key Stages of the Route

The Camino Portugués is typically divided into stages, with each stage representing a day's walk. Here are the key stages along the route from Porto:

1.Porto to Vilarinho (27 km)

Highlights: Leaving the historic city of Porto, crossing the Douro River, and walking through the Portuguese countryside.

2.Vilarinho to Barcelos (20 km)

Highlights: The medieval town of Barcelos, famous for its pottery and the iconic Barcelos rooster.

3.Barcelos to Ponte de Lima (34 km)

Highlights: Walking through vineyards and forests, reaching Ponte de Lima, the oldest town in Portugal with a beautiful Roman bridge.

4.Ponte de Lima to Rubiães (18 km)

Highlights: The challenging ascent through the Labruja mountains, offering stunning views and a sense of accomplishment.

5.Rubiães to Tui (19 km)

Highlights: Crossing into Spain at the town of Valença, with its impressive fortress, and arriving in Tui, home to a beautiful cathedral.

6.Tui to O Porriño (16 km)

Highlights: Walking through the Galician countryside and enjoying the lush landscapes.

7.O Porriño to Redondela (15 km)

Highlights: The small town of Redondela, known for its viaducts and proximity to the coast.

8.Redondela to Pontevedra (20 km)

Highlights: The historic city of Pontevedra, with its well-preserved old town and numerous churches.

9.Pontevedra to Caldas de Reis (21 km)

Highlights: The spa town of Caldas de Reis, famous for its hot springs and relaxing atmosphere.

10.Caldas de Reis to Padrón (19 km)

Highlights: The town of Padrón, linked to the legend of St. James and known for its delicious peppers (pimientos de Padrón).

11.Padrón to Santiago de Compostela (25 km)

Highlights: The final stretch to Santiago de Compostela, the emotional arrival at the cathedral, and attending the Pilgrim's Mass.

Terrain and Scenery

The Camino Portugués offers a mix of urban and rural landscapes, with sections through historic cities, charming villages, vineyards, forests, and coastal areas. The terrain is generally less challenging than the Camino Francés, with fewer steep climbs, making it accessible to a wider range of pilgrims.

Cultural Experience

Walking the Camino Portugués provides a rich cultural experience, allowing pilgrims to immerse themselves in both Portuguese and Galician traditions, cuisine, and hospitality. From the vibrant fado music of Lisbon to the traditional pilgrim dishes in Galicia, the route offers a diverse and enriching journey.

Practical Information

Accommodation: A mix of albergues, guesthouses, and hotels are available along the route, with many options catering specifically to pilgrims.

Weather: The best times to walk are spring (April to June) and autumn (September to October) for mild temperatures and fewer crowds.

Pilgrim Passport: Ensure you carry your pilgrim passport to access accommodation and collect stamps along the way.

The Camino Portugués offers a unique and fulfilling pilgrimage experience, blending the rich cultural heritage of Portugal and Spain with the spiritual journey to Santiago de Compostela. Whether you start in Lisbon or Porto, this route promises a memorable and transformative adventure.

Highlights and Points of Interest

The Camino Portugués is rich in cultural, historical, and natural landmarks. Here are some of the highlights and points of interest you should not miss along the route:

From Lisbon

Lisbon:

Jerónimos Monastery: A UNESCO World Heritage Site, this stunning monastery is a prime example of Manueline architecture.

Belém Tower: Another UNESCO site, offering a glimpse into Portugal's Age of Discoveries.

Alfama and Bairro Alto: Historic neighborhoods known for their narrow streets, fado music, and vibrant nightlife.

Santarém:

Gothic Cathedral: Known for its stunning architecture and rich history.

Portas do Sol: Offers panoramic views of the Tagus River and surrounding countryside.

Tomar:

Convent of Christ: A UNESCO World Heritage Site and former Templar stronghold with intricate Manueline details.

Aqueduct of Pegões: An impressive aqueduct built to supply water to the convent.

Coimbra:

University of Coimbra: One of the oldest universities in Europe with a stunning library, Joanina Library.

Monastery of Santa Cruz: The resting place of Portugal's first two kings.

From Porto

Porto:

Ribeira District: A UNESCO World Heritage site with narrow streets, colorful buildings, and lively atmosphere along the Douro River.

Dom Luís I Bridge: An iconic iron bridge offering spectacular views of the city and river.

Livraria Lello: One of the most beautiful bookstores in the world, known for its stunning interior and historic significance.

Ponte de Lima:

Roman Bridge: A beautifully preserved bridge over the Lima River, and the town itself is the oldest in Portugal.

Festival of Vaca das Cordas: A unique and lively local festival

Valença:

Fortress of Valença: An impressive fortification with panoramic views and a charming old town.

Tui:

Tui Cathedral: A beautiful cathedral with Gothic and Romanesque elements, offering insights into the region's religious history.

Redondela:

Viaducts: Known for its striking railway viaducts that dominate the skyline.

Pontevedra:

Church of the Pilgrim Virgin: A unique scallop-shell-shaped church that is a must-see for pilgrims.

Historic Old Town: Well-preserved and pedestrian-friendly, perfect for a relaxing stroll.

Caldas de Reis:

Thermal Springs: Enjoy a soak in the natural hot springs, which have been used since Roman times.

Church of Santa María: An interesting historical site with beautiful architecture.

Padrón:

Iglesia de Santiago: Where, according to legend, the boat carrying St. James's body was moored.

Padrón Peppers: Try the famous local delicacy, pimientos de Padrón.

Santiago de Compostela:

Cathedral of Santiago de Compostela: The final destination of the pilgrimage, home to the remains of St. James. Don't miss the Pilgrim's Mass and the Botafumeiro.

Plaza del Obradoiro: The grand square in front of the cathedral, a place of celebration and reflection for pilgrims.

Museum of the Galician People: Offers insights into the culture, history, and traditions of Galicia.

Natural and Scenic Highlights

Labruja Mountains:

A challenging but rewarding ascent offering stunning views of the surrounding landscape.

Galician Countryside:

Known for its lush greenery, rolling hills, and picturesque villages. Walking through this region offers a peaceful and scenic experience.

River Crossings:

Numerous crossings over charming old bridges, providing beautiful photo opportunities and moments of tranquility.

Coastal Views:

In some sections, particularly near Redondela, you can enjoy views of the Atlantic coast and the Ría de Vigo.

The Camino Portugués offers a rich tapestry of experiences, from historic cities and quaint villages to beautiful natural landscapes and cultural landmarks. Each stop along the way provides unique insights and memories, making the pilgrimage a deeply enriching journey.

Insider Tips for a Smooth Journey

Walking the Camino Portugués is a rewarding and transformative experience, but it requires some planning and preparation to ensure a smooth journey. Here are some insider tips to help you make the most of your pilgrimage:

1. Preparing for the Journey

Physical Training:

Start training a few months before your departure. Include long walks, preferably with a loaded backpack, to build stamina and get used to carrying your gear.

Footwear:

Invest in high-quality, well-broken-in hiking boots or shoes. Ensure they provide good support and are comfortable for long distances.

Packing:

Pack light but ensure you have all the essentials. Use a checklist to avoid overpacking. Remember, a lighter backpack makes for a more enjoyable walk.

2. Planning Your Route

Stages:

Plan your daily stages based on your fitness level and the availability of accommodation. Allow for flexibility in your schedule to account for rest days or unexpected delays.

Maps and Guides:

Carry a reliable guidebook or use apps specifically designed for the Camino. They provide useful information about the route, accommodation, and points of interest.

3. Accommodation Tips

Booking:

During peak seasons (spring and autumn), it's advisable to book your accommodation in advance, especially in popular towns.

For municipal albergues that operate on a first-come, first-served basis, try to arrive early in the afternoon to secure a bed.

Types of Accommodation:

Experience a mix of accommodation options, from albergues and guesthouses to hotels and casa rurales. Each offers a different experience and comfort level.

Facilities:

Check if the albergue or hostel has laundry facilities, Wi-Fi, and kitchen access. These can make your stay more comfortable.

4. Dining and Nutrition

Pilgrim Menus:

Take advantage of the Pilgrim's Menu (Menú del Peregrino) offered by many restaurants. It's a cost-effective way to enjoy a three-course meal, including wine or water.

Local Cuisine:

Try regional specialties along the way, such as bacalhau (salt cod) in Portugal and pulpo a la gallega (Galician octopus) in Spain.

Snacks:

Carry snacks like nuts, dried fruits, and energy bars to keep your energy up during long walks.

Hydration:

Drink plenty of water, especially during the hotter months. Use a refillable water bottle and take advantage of fountains along the route.

5. Health and Safety

Foot Care:

Take good care of your feet. Apply blister prevention methods, keep your feet clean and dry, and rest at the first sign of discomfort.

First Aid Kit:

Carry a basic first aid kit including band-aids, blister pads, antiseptic wipes, pain relievers, and any personal medications.

Sunscreen and Hat:

Protect yourself from the sun by applying sunscreen regularly and wearing a hat.

Emergency Contacts:

Keep a list of emergency contacts, including local medical facilities and the emergency number (112) in Portugal and Spain.

6. Cultural Etiquette

Language:

Learn a few basic phrases in Portuguese and Spanish. Locals appreciate the effort and it can help you navigate daily interactions more smoothly.

Respect Local Customs:

Be respectful of local customs and traditions. Dress modestly when visiting churches and religious sites.

Quiet Hours:

Be mindful of quiet hours in albergues, usually between 10 PM and 6 AM. Respecting these helps everyone get a good night's rest.

7. Navigating the Route

Waymarking:

The Camino Portugués is well-marked with yellow arrows and scallop shell symbols. Pay attention to these markers to stay on the right path.

Alternative Routes:

Be aware of alternative routes that might offer different experiences. For example, the Coastal Route (Camino Portugués de la Costa) offers beautiful seaside views.

Daily Routine:

Start walking early in the morning to avoid the midday heat and to secure your accommodation in the next town.

8. Staying Connected

Wi-Fi and Internet:

Most accommodations offer Wi-Fi, but it might be limited. Consider buying a local SIM card for more reliable internet access.

Charging Devices:

Carry a portable charger to ensure your phone and other devices remain charged, especially if you use them for navigation and communication.

9. Enjoying the Journey

Pace Yourself:

Walk at a pace that's comfortable for you. Listen to your body and take breaks as needed.

Embrace the Experience:

Engage with fellow pilgrims, savor local foods, and take in the beautiful landscapes. The journey is as important as the destination.

Reflection:

Take time for personal reflection and enjoy the spiritual aspects of the pilgrimage. Many pilgrims find the journey transformative and deeply meaningful.

By following these insider tips, you can ensure a smooth and enjoyable pilgrimage on the Camino Portugués. Preparation, respect for local customs, and a flexible approach will help you make the most of this incredible journey.

Chapter 5

The Camino del Norte:

Overview of the Route

The Camino del Norte, also known as the Northern Way, is a scenic and historically significant route of the Camino de Santiago. This route follows the northern coast of Spain, offering stunning coastal views, lush landscapes, and a blend of cultural and historical experiences. The Camino del Norte spans approximately 825 kilometers (513 miles) from Irún, near the French border, to the cathedral of Santiago de Compostela. Here is an in-depth overview of the Camino del Norte:

Starting Point

Irún:

Location: A charming town situated on the border between Spain and France, marking the beginning of the Camino del Norte.

Highlights: The historic town center, the Church of Nuestra Señora del Juncal, and the scenic Bidasoa River.

Key Stages of the Route

The Camino del Norte is typically divided into stages, with each stage representing a day's walk. Here are the key stages along the route:

1.Irún to San Sebastián (27 km)

Highlights: Walking along the stunning coastline, arriving at the beautiful city of San Sebastián known for its beaches, pintxos (Basque tapas), and vibrant old town.

2. San Sebastián to Zarautz (22 km)

Highlights: Coastal views, the picturesque town of Zarautz with its long beach and surf culture.

3. Zarautz to Deba (21 km)

Highlights: Rolling hills, vineyards, and the charming seaside town of Deba.

4. Deba to Markina-Xemein (24 km)

Highlights: Rural landscapes, small villages, and traditional Basque architecture.

5. Markina-Xemein to Gernika (25 km)

Highlights: The historic town of Gernika, known for its oak tree symbolizing Basque freedom and the Gernika Peace Museum.

6. Gernika to Bilbao (30 km)

Highlights: Entering the vibrant city of Bilbao, home to the iconic Guggenheim Museum, and rich cultural offerings.

7. Bilbao to Portugalete (11 km)

Highlights: A short stage along the Nervión River, crossing the Vizcaya Bridge, a UNESCO World Heritage Site.

8. Portugalete to Castro Urdiales (27 km)

Highlights: Coastal paths, arriving in the historic town of Castro Urdiales with its Gothic church and medieval castle.

9. Castro Urdiales to Laredo (26 km)

Highlights: Beautiful beaches, coastal cliffs, and the old town of Laredo.

10. Laredo to Güemes (28 km)

Highlights: Scenic countryside, charming villages, and the welcoming albergue in Güemes.

11. Güemes to Santander (11 km)

Highlights: Arriving in the bustling city of Santander, known for its beautiful bay, historic buildings, and cultural sites.

12. Santander to Santillana del Mar (37 km)

Highlights: Walking through picturesque villages, arriving in the medieval village of Santillana del Mar with its cobblestone streets and historic architecture.

13. Santillana del Mar to Comillas (22 km)

Highlights: Scenic coastal paths, the charming town of Comillas with Gaudí's El Capricho and the Pontifical University.

14. Comillas to Colombres (28 km)

Highlights: Coastal and rural landscapes, crossing into the Asturias region.

15. Colombres to Llanes (23 km)

Highlights: Beautiful beaches, the historic town of Llanes with its medieval walls and harbor.

16. Llanes to Ribadesella (30 km)

Highlights: Stunning coastal views, the seaside town of Ribadesella known for its prehistoric caves and beach.

17. Ribadesella to Sebrayo (32 km)

Highlights: Coastal and rural paths, passing through traditional Asturian villages.

18. Sebrayo to Gijón (36 km)

Highlights: Entering the lively city of Gijón, known for its maritime heritage, beaches, and cultural attractions.

19. Gijón to Avilés (25 km)

Highlights: Coastal paths, the historic town of Avilés with its well-preserved old quarter and modern Niemeyer Center.

20. Avilés to Muros de Nalón (21 km)

Highlights: Scenic rural landscapes and the peaceful village of Muros de Nalón.

21. Muros de Nalón to Soto de Luiña (16 km)

Highlights: Beautiful countryside and the small village of Soto de Luiña.

22. Soto de Luiña to Cadavedo (24 km)

Highlights: Coastal and rural paths, the quaint village of Cadavedo.

23. Cadavedo to Luarca (16 km)

Highlights: Scenic coastal paths, arriving in the fishing village of Luarca known for its picturesque harbor.

25. Luarca to La Caridad (29 km)

Highlights: Walking through rural landscapes and traditional Asturian villages.

25. La Caridad to Ribadeo (22 km)

Highlights: Crossing into the Galicia region, the coastal town of Ribadeo with its historic center.

26. Ribadeo to Lourenzá (29 km)

Highlights: Rural Galicia, the monastery of San Salvador in Lourenzá.

27. Lourenzá to Abadín (26 km)

Highlights: Walking through green valleys and rural villages.

28. Abadín to Vilalba (20 km)

Highlights: Scenic countryside and the historic town of Vilalba.

29. Vilalba to Baamonde (18 km)

Highlights: Rural landscapes and the peaceful village of Baamonde.

30. Baamonde to Sobrado dos Monxes (40 km)

Highlights: The Monastery of Sobrado, a significant historical and religious site.

31. Sobrado dos Monxes to Arzúa (22 km)

Highlights: Joining the Camino Francés, the town of Arzúa known for its cheese.

32. Arzúa to Pedrouzo (19 km)

Highlights: Walking through forests and small villages, nearing the final destination.

33. Pedrouzo to Santiago de Compostela (20 km)

Highlights: The final stretch to Santiago de Compostela, the emotional arrival at the cathedral, and attending the Pilgrim's Mass.

Key Landmarks and Destinations

San Sebastián: Known for its beautiful beaches, vibrant old town, and world-renowned culinary scene.

Bilbao: Home to the iconic Guggenheim Museum, the historic Casco Viejo (Old Quarter), and a rich cultural scene.

Santillana del Mar: A medieval village with cobblestone streets, historic buildings, and the Collegiate Church of Santa Juliana.

Gijón: A lively coastal city with a beautiful beach, historic sites, and cultural attractions.

Ribadesella: Famous for its prehistoric caves, beautiful beach, and picturesque harbor.

Avilés: Known for its well-preserved old quarter and the modern Niemeyer Center.

Luarca: A charming fishing village with a picturesque harbor and traditional Asturian architecture.

Ribadeo: A coastal town with a historic center and beautiful views of the estuary.

Santiago de Compostela: The final destination, featuring the magnificent cathedral where the remains of

St. James are believed to be buried, and the bustling Plaza del Obradoiro.

Terrain and Scenery

The Camino del Norte offers a mix of coastal and inland scenery, with stunning beaches, rugged cliffs, lush forests, and rolling hills. The terrain is more challenging than some other routes, with frequent ascents and descents, but the breathtaking views and diverse landscapes make it a rewarding journey.

Cultural Experience

Walking the Camino del Norte provides a rich cultural experience, allowing pilgrims to immerse themselves in Basque, Cantabrian, Asturian, and Galician traditions, cuisine, and hospitality. From the pintxos bars of San Sebastián to the seafood dishes of Galicia, the route offers a diverse and enriching journey.

Practical Information

Accommodation: A mix of albergues, guesthouses, and hotels are available along the route, with many options catering specifically to pilgrims.

Weather: The best times to walk are spring (April to June) and autumn (September to October) for mild temperatures and fewer crowds.

Pilgrim Passport: Ensure you carry your pilgrim passport to access accommodation and collect stamps along the way.

The Camino del Norte offers a unique and fulfilling pilgrimage experience, blending the stunning coastal scenery of northern Spain with the spiritual journey to Santiago de Compostela. Whether you are drawn by the natural beauty, cultural richness, or personal challenge, this route promises a memorable and transformative adventure.

Coastal Beauty and Challenges

The Camino del Norte, or the Northern Way, is renowned for its stunning coastal landscapes and the diverse challenges it presents to pilgrims. Walking this route provides an unparalleled opportunity to experience the beauty of Spain's northern coast while facing the physical and logistical challenges that come with it. Here's a detailed look at the coastal beauty and challenges of the Camino del Norte:

Coastal Beauty

1. Breathtaking Coastal Views:

San Sebastián: One of the most beautiful cities on the route, known for its pristine beaches such as La Concha and Zurriola. The coastal path offers stunning views of the Bay of Biscay.

Zarautz: Famous for its long sandy beach and surf culture, this town provides picturesque coastal scenery and a lively atmosphere.

Llanes: This coastal town boasts dramatic cliffs, beautiful beaches like Playa de Toro, and historic architecture, offering scenic views along the coast.

Ribadesella: Known for its prehistoric caves and the stunning Playa de Santa Marina, this seaside town offers both natural beauty and historical interest.

Gijón: A vibrant city with urban beaches such as Playa de San Lorenzo, blending coastal charm with cultural attractions.

Ribadeo: The entry point into Galicia, offering spectacular views of the estuary and the famous As Catedrais beach with its natural rock formations.

2. Scenic Coastal Walks:

Cliffs and Headlands: The route often takes you along rugged cliffs and headlands, providing dramatic and uninterrupted views of the sea.

Fishing Villages: Picturesque fishing villages such as Luarca and Cudillero offer charming, postcard-perfect settings with colorful houses and bustling harbors.

Lush Green Landscapes: The verdant countryside contrasts beautifully with the blue of the ocean, especially in the regions of Asturias and Galicia.

3. Unique Natural Features:

Beaches and Coves: Numerous sandy beaches and hidden coves along the route provide perfect spots for rest and relaxation.

Natural Parks: The route passes through or near several natural parks, such as the Urdaibai Biosphere Reserve, which offers rich biodiversity and stunning scenery.

Challenges

1. Physical Demands:

Elevation Changes: The Camino del Norte features frequent and significant elevation changes. Pilgrims will encounter many ascents and descents as they traverse coastal cliffs and mountainous terrain.

Long Distances: Some stages are relatively long, requiring good physical endurance. Preparing with regular walking and conditioning is essential.

2. Weather Conditions:

Variable Weather: The northern coast of Spain experiences varied weather conditions, including rain, wind, and cooler temperatures, even in summer. Pilgrims should be prepared for sudden weather changes.

Coastal Winds: Walking along the coast can expose you to strong winds, which can be challenging and tiring over long distances.

3. Navigation:

Waymarking: While the Camino del Norte is generally well-marked, there can be sections where waymarking is less clear. It's essential to carry a reliable guidebook or use a Camino-specific navigation app.

Alternative Routes: Some sections offer alternative inland routes to avoid difficult coastal paths or weather conditions. Knowing when to take these alternatives can be crucial for safety and comfort.

4. Accommodation Logistics:

Availability: While there are many albergues and accommodations along the route, some areas, particularly in rural sections, have limited options. Planning and sometimes booking in advance is advisable, especially during peak seasons.

Facilities: Coastal towns can get crowded during the summer months due to tourism, so securing accommodation early in the day is important.

5. Mental and Emotional Challenges:

Loneliness and Isolation: The Camino del Norte is less traveled than the Camino Francés, meaning fewer fellow pilgrims and potentially more isolation. While some may enjoy the solitude, others may find it challenging.

Monotony in Long Stretches: Despite the beautiful scenery, long stretches of walking, especially in less populated areas, can become monotonous and mentally taxing.

Tips for Overcoming Challenges

Preparation:

Start training a few months before your departure, focusing on building stamina and strength for long walks and elevation changes.

Ensure your footwear is well-broken-in and suitable for varied terrains.

Packing:

Pack light but include essential items such as a good rain jacket, layers for variable weather, and a reliable guidebook or navigation app.

Carry snacks and sufficient water, especially in remote areas where services may be limited.

Accommodation Planning:

Book accommodations in advance during peak seasons or in areas with limited options.

Arrive early in the afternoon to secure a bed in albergues, especially in popular coastal towns.

Mental Preparation:

Embrace the solitude and use it as an opportunity for reflection and personal growth.

Stay connected with fellow pilgrims and locals to combat feelings of loneliness.

Flexibility:

Be prepared to take alternative routes if weather conditions are unfavorable or if the coastal path proves too challenging.

Allow for rest days to recover and enjoy the journey at a comfortable pace.

The Camino del Norte is a journey of remarkable beauty and considerable challenge. By preparing well and embracing both the physical and mental demands, you can fully appreciate the stunning coastal landscapes and the rich cultural experiences this route offers.

Important Stops and Cultural Insights

The Camino del Norte is not only a journey through breathtaking coastal landscapes but also a path rich in cultural and historical significance. Here are some of the most important stops along the route and the cultural insights they offer:

Important Stops

1. Irún

Highlights: The starting point of the Camino del Norte, known for its historic center, the Church of Nuestra Señora del Juncal, and the scenic Bidasoa River.

Cultural Insights: Irún is part of the Basque Country, a region with a distinct language and culture. The Basque people have a rich history of maritime activities and unique traditions.

2. San Sebastián (Donostia)

Highlights: Famous for its beautiful beaches like La Concha, vibrant old town, and world-renowned culinary scene, especially the pintxos bars.

Cultural Insights: San Sebastián is a cultural hub in the Basque Country, known for its festivals such as the San Sebastián International Film Festival and its unique Basque cuisine.

3. Zarautz

Highlights: Known for its long sandy beach, surf culture, and picturesque coastal views.

Cultural Insights: Zarautz offers insights into the Basque coastal lifestyle, with a strong emphasis on fishing and surfing.

4. Bilbao

Highlights: Home to the iconic Guggenheim Museum, the historic Casco Viejo (Old Quarter), and a vibrant arts scene.

Cultural Insights: Bilbao is a prime example of urban regeneration, blending modern architecture with traditional Basque culture. It's a city of contrasts where the old meets the new.

5. Santander

Highlights: The bustling capital of Cantabria, known for its beautiful bay, historic buildings, and cultural sites such as the Centro Botín.

Cultural Insights: Santander offers a mix of maritime history and modern urban development. The city's maritime museum provides a deep dive into Cantabria's seafaring heritage.

6. Santillana del Mar

Highlights: A medieval village with cobblestone streets, historic buildings, and the Collegiate Church of Santa Juliana.

Cultural Insights: Often called the "town of three lies" (it's not holy, flat, or by the sea), Santillana del Mar is a well-preserved example of medieval architecture and culture.

7. Comillas

Highlights: Known for Gaudí's El Capricho, the Pontifical University, and beautiful coastal scenery.

Cultural Insights: Comillas reflects the influence of the Spanish aristocracy and its connection to modernist architecture through Gaudí's work.

8. Llanes

Highlights: A picturesque coastal town with medieval walls, a charming harbor, and beautiful beaches like Playa de Toro.

Cultural Insights: Llanes has a rich maritime tradition and is famous for its folklore, festivals, and the unique bufón phenomenon (sea geysers).

9. Gijón

Highlights: A lively coastal city known for its maritime heritage, beaches, and cultural attractions such as the Laboral City of Culture.

Cultural Insights: Gijón is a city where industrial history meets cultural innovation, offering a glimpse into Asturian life and traditions.

10. Ribadesella

Highlights: Famous for its prehistoric caves (Tito Bustillo Cave), beautiful beach, and scenic harbor.

Cultural Insights: Ribadesella is known for its prehistoric art and the annual Descenso Internacional del Sella, a major canoeing event that attracts international participants.

11. Avilés

Highlights: A historic town with a well-preserved old quarter and the modern Niemeyer Center.

Cultural Insights: Avilés showcases a blend of medieval charm and modern architectural innovation, reflecting the region's industrial past and cultural renaissance.

12. Luarca

Highlights: A charming fishing village with a picturesque harbor and traditional Asturian architecture.

Cultural Insights: Luarca is known for its connection to the sea, offering insights into the fishing traditions and maritime culture of Asturias.

13. Ribadeo

Highlights: A coastal town marking the entry into Galicia, known for its historic center and the spectacular As Catedrais beach with its natural rock formations.

Cultural Insights: Ribadeo blends Galician and Asturian influences, showcasing a rich maritime heritage and stunning natural beauty.

14. Santiago de Compostela

Highlights: The final destination of the pilgrimage, featuring the magnificent cathedral where the remains of St. James are believed to be buried, and the bustling Plaza del Obradoiro.

Cultural Insights: Santiago de Compostela is a spiritual and cultural hub, attracting pilgrims from all over the world. The city's historic center is a UNESCO World Heritage site, rich in history, architecture, and religious significance.

Cultural Insights Along the Route

Basque Country:

Language: The Basque language (Euskara) is distinct from Spanish and has no known linguistic relatives. Learning a few basic phrases can enhance your experience.

Cuisine: Basque cuisine is renowned for its quality and creativity. Pintxos, small bar snacks, are a must-try, and the region's seafood is exceptional.

Festivals: Basque festivals, such as Semana Grande in San Sebastián, are lively and showcase traditional music, dance, and sports.

Cantabria:

History: The region is known for its prehistoric caves, including Altamira, often called the "Sistine Chapel of Prehistoric Art."

Music and Dance: Traditional Cantabrian music and dance, including the popular jota, are integral to local culture.

Asturias:

Cider Culture: Asturias is famous for its cider (sidra). Visit a sidrería to experience the unique way cider is poured and enjoyed.

Folklore: Asturian folklore is rich with tales of mythological creatures like the xana (water fairy) and the trasgu (mischievous goblin).

Galicia:

Language: Galician (Galego) is widely spoken and shares similarities with Portuguese. It's helpful to learn a few phrases.

Pilgrimage Tradition: The Camino de Santiago is deeply embedded in Galician culture. The region is known for its hospitality towards pilgrims.

Cuisine: Galician cuisine is renowned for its seafood, especially pulpo a la gallega (Galician octopus) and empanadas.

Local Markets and Artisan Products:

Along the route, you'll find numerous local markets offering fresh produce, artisanal cheeses, cured meats, and handmade crafts. Engaging with local vendors provides a deeper understanding of the region's agricultural and artisanal traditions.

Religious and Historical Sites:

The route is dotted with churches, monasteries, and historical landmarks that offer insights into the region's religious and historical significance. Visiting these sites can provide a richer context for your journey.

The Camino del Norte is a journey through diverse cultures and histories, offering pilgrims a chance to immerse themselves in the unique traditions, cuisines, and landscapes of northern Spain. Each stop along the way provides opportunities to learn, experience, and appreciate the rich cultural tapestry of this remarkable route.

Accommodation and Dining Recommendations

Ensuring comfortable accommodation and enjoying the local cuisine are key aspects of a rewarding pilgrimage on the Camino del Norte. Here are some recommendations for both accommodation and dining along the route:

Accommodation Recommendations

1. Irún

Albergue de Peregrinos de Irún: A basic but welcoming pilgrim hostel, providing a good start to the journey.

Hotel Alcázar: For more comfort, this hotel offers clean rooms and a pleasant garden.

2. San Sebastián

Albergue de Peregrinos La Sirena: Located close to the beach, this albergue is a popular choice among pilgrims.

Pensión Amaiur: A charming guesthouse in the old town, offering a comfortable stay with a personal touch.

3. Zarautz

Albergue de Peregrinos de Zarautz: A well-maintained albergue with friendly staff and good facilities.

Hotel Alameda: A cozy hotel near the beach, known for its comfortable rooms and excellent service.

4. Bilbao

Albergue Bilbao Aterpetxea: A modern hostel with good amenities, located a short distance from the city center.

Hotel Gran Bilbao: A stylish hotel offering spacious rooms and excellent breakfast options.

5. Santander

Albergue de Peregrinos La Pereda: A simple albergue with all the necessary amenities for a comfortable stay.

Hotel Bahía: Centrally located with beautiful views of the bay, this hotel offers luxury and comfort.

6. Santillana del Mar

Albergue Solar de Hidalgos: A historic building offering a unique and charming stay for pilgrims.

Parador de Santillana Gil Blas: A luxurious option located in a charming manor house, perfect for a splurge.

7. Comillas

Albergue El Peregrino: A popular choice among pilgrims, offering a warm and welcoming atmosphere.

Abba Comillas Golf Hotel: Offers a more upscale stay with beautiful views and excellent facilities.

8. Llanes

Albergue La Casona del Peregrino: A well-located albergue with good facilities and a friendly atmosphere.

Hotel Don Paco: A comfortable hotel situated in a renovated convent, offering a peaceful stay.

9. Gijón

Albergue de Peregrinos de Gijón: A modern albergue with all the necessary amenities.

NH Gijón: A beachfront hotel with stylish rooms and excellent services.

10. Ribadesella

Albergue Roberto Frassinelli: A welcoming albergue with good facilities and a great location near the beach.

Hotel Villa Rosario: A beautiful hotel offering luxurious rooms and stunning views of the sea.

11. Avilés

Albergue de Peregrinos Pedro Solís: A centrally located albergue with a warm and friendly atmosphere.

Hotel 40 Nudos: Offers comfortable rooms and a convenient location near the old town.

12. Luarca

Albergue Alberguería de Luarca: A modern and well-equipped albergue with a welcoming staff.

Hotel Villa de Luarca: A charming hotel with comfortable rooms and a central location.

13. Ribadeo

Albergue de Peregrinos de Ribadeo: A clean and comfortable albergue with good facilities.

Parador de Ribadeo: Offers stunning views of the estuary and a luxurious stay.

14. Santiago de Compostela

Albergue Seminario Menor: A large albergue located in a historic building, offering a unique experience.

Parador de Santiago - Hostal dos Reis Católicos: A luxurious hotel located right next to the cathedral, providing an unforgettable stay.

Dining Recommendations

1. Irún

Bodegon Joxe Mari: Known for its excellent Basque cuisine and warm atmosphere.

Restaurante Sugaar: Offers traditional dishes with a modern twist.

2. San Sebastián

Bar Néstor: Famous for its incredible tortilla de patatas and juicy steaks.

La Viña: Known for its legendary cheesecake and delicious pintxos.

3. Zarautz

Karlos Arguiñano: A beachfront restaurant offering a wide variety of Basque dishes.

Restaurante Otzarreta: Known for its fresh seafood and traditional Basque cuisine.

4. Bilbao

La Vina del Ensanche: A traditional tavern offering excellent pintxos and local wines.

Café Iruña: A historic café known for its beautiful interior and delicious tapas.

5. Santander

La Bombi: Famous for its fresh seafood and traditional Cantabrian dishes.

Cañadío: Known for its excellent tapas and vibrant atmosphere.

6. Santillana del Mar

El Castillo: Offers traditional Cantabrian dishes in a cozy setting.

Parador de Santillana: Known for its refined regional cuisine and historic ambiance.

7. Comillas

Restaurante El Galeón: Offers a variety of seafood dishes and traditional Cantabrian cuisine.

Gurea: Known for its friendly service and delicious local dishes.

8. Llanes

El Cuera: A popular restaurant offering fresh seafood and traditional Asturian dishes.

Casa Canene: Known for its friendly atmosphere and hearty portions.

9. Gijón

Casa Trabanco: A cider house offering traditional Asturian dishes and locally-produced cider.

La Galana: Known for its excellent seafood and lively atmosphere.

10. Ribadesella

El Campanu: Famous for its seafood dishes and beautiful views of the harbor.

La Chopera: Offers a variety of traditional Asturian dishes in a cozy setting.

11. Avilés

Tierra Astur: A popular cider house offering a wide variety of Asturian dishes and local cider.

Ronda 14: Known for its fusion of Asturian and Japanese cuisine.

12. Luarca

La Farola: Offers fresh seafood and traditional Asturian dishes with a modern twist.

El Barómetro: Known for its friendly atmosphere and delicious local cuisine.

13. Ribadeo

La Botellería: Famous for its seafood and traditional Galician dishes.

O Cabazo: Offers a variety of regional specialties and beautiful views of the estuary.

14. Santiago de Compostela

Casa Marcelo: A Michelin-starred restaurant known for its innovative Galician cuisine.

O Gato Negro: Famous for its fresh seafood and traditional Galician tapas.

By following these accommodation and dining recommendations, you can ensure a comfortable and enjoyable experience on the Camino del Norte.

Chapter 6

Lesser-Known Routes

The Via de la Plata

The Via de la Plata, or the Silver Way, is one of the lesser-known routes of the Camino de Santiago, but it offers a unique and enriching pilgrimage experience. This ancient route stretches approximately 1,000 kilometers (620 miles) from Seville in the south of Spain to Santiago de Compostela in the northwest. The Via de la Plata is renowned for its historical significance, diverse landscapes, and fewer crowds compared to other Camino routes. Here is an in-depth overview of the Via de la Plata:

Overview of the Route

Starting Point: Seville

Location: The journey begins in the vibrant city of Seville, the capital of Andalusia.

Highlights: Seville is known for its stunning architecture, flamenco music, and rich cultural heritage. Key sites include the Seville Cathedral, the Alcázar, and Plaza de España.

Key Stages of the Route

The Via de la Plata is typically divided into stages, with each stage representing a day's walk. Here are the key stages along the route:

1.Seville to Guillena (22 km)

Highlights: Leaving the historic city of Seville, walking through olive groves and fields, and arriving in the small town of Guillena.

2. Guillena to Castilblanco de los Arroyos (19 km)

Highlights: Rural landscapes, rolling hills, and the tranquil town of Castilblanco de los Arroyos.

3. Castilblanco de los Arroyos to Almadén de la Plata (29 km)

Highlights: Passing through Sierra Norte Natural Park, scenic views, and the charming village of Almadén de la Plata.

4. Almadén de la Plata to Monesterio (34 km)

Highlights: Entering the region of Extremadura, walking through forests and pastures, and arriving in Monesterio, known for its ham production.

5. Monesterio to Fuente de Cantos (21 km)

Highlights: Rural scenery, traditional villages, and the town of Fuente de Cantos.

6. Fuente de Cantos to Zafra (25 km)

Highlights: Vineyards and olive groves, the historic town of Zafra with its beautiful Plaza Grande and Alcázar.

7. Zafra to Villafranca de los Barros (20 km)

Highlights: Rolling countryside, vineyards, and the friendly town of Villafranca de los Barros.

8. Villafranca de los Barros to Torremejía (27 km)

Highlights: Flat, open landscapes, and the quiet village of Torremejía.

9. Torremejía to Mérida (16 km)

Highlights: Arriving in the historic city of Mérida, known for its well-preserved Roman ruins including the Roman Theatre and Amphitheatre.

10. Mérida to Aljucén (17 km)

Highlights: Roman aqueducts, rural paths, and the small village of Aljucén.

11. Aljucén to Alcuéscar (21 km)

Highlights: Walking through forests and pastures, and reaching the town of Alcuéscar with its beautiful church.

12. Alcuéscar to Cáceres (37 km)

Highlights: The long stage to the UNESCO World Heritage city of Cáceres, known for its medieval old town and historic architecture.

13. Cáceres to Casar de Cáceres (11 km)

Highlights: A shorter stage through rural landscapes to the town of Casar de Cáceres, known for its Torta del Casar cheese.

14. Casar de Cáceres to Cañaveral (35 km)

Highlights: Scenic countryside, traditional villages, and the town of Cañaveral.

15. Cañaveral to Galisteo (27 km)

Highlights: Beautiful landscapes, the historic walled town of Galisteo with its unique architecture.

16. Galisteo to Carcaboso (13 km)

Highlights: A short walk through rural areas to the village of Carcaboso.

17. Carcaboso to Aldeanueva del Camino (38 km)

Highlights: A long stage through the picturesque landscapes of Extremadura, arriving in Aldeanueva del Camino.

18. Aldeanueva del Camino to Baños de Montemayor (22 km)

Highlights: Walking through the beautiful Ambroz Valley and the spa town of Baños de Montemayor.

19. Baños de Montemayor to Fuenterroble de Salvatierra (32 km)

Highlights: Entering the region of Castilla y León, and the friendly village of Fuenterroble de Salvatierra.

20. Fuenterroble de Salvatierra to San Pedro de Rozados (28 km)

Highlights: Scenic countryside and the quiet village of San Pedro de Rozados.

21. San Pedro de Rozados to Salamanca (24 km)

Highlights: Arriving in the historic city of Salamanca, known for its beautiful Plaza Mayor, university, and cathedrals.

22. Salamanca to Calzada de Valdunciel (15 km)

Highlights: A shorter stage through rural landscapes to the village of Calzada de Valdunciel.

23. Calzada de Valdunciel to El Cubo de la Tierra del Vino (20 km)

Highlights: Walking through vineyards and countryside, arriving in El Cubo de la Tierra del Vino.

24. El Cubo de la Tierra del Vino to Zamora (32 km)

Highlights: Reaching the historic city of Zamora, known for its Romanesque architecture and medieval castle.

25. Zamora to Montamarta (18 km)

Highlights: Scenic rural landscapes and the small village of Montamarta.

26. Montamarta to Granja de Moreruela (22 km)

Highlights: Walking through peaceful countryside to the village of Granja de Moreruela.

27. Granja de Moreruela to Benavente (25 km)

Highlights: Scenic landscapes and the historic town of Benavente with its impressive castle.

28. Benavente to Alija del Infantado (20 km)

Highlights: Rural paths and the charming village of Alija del Infantado.

29. Alija del Infantado to La Bañeza (18 km)

Highlights: Rolling countryside and the lively town of La Bañeza.

30. La Bañeza to Astorga (24 km)

Highlights: Arriving in the historic town of Astorga, known for its Gaudí-designed Episcopal Palace and beautiful cathedral.

31. Astorga to Rabanal del Camino (20 km)

Highlights: Starting the ascent into the mountains, the picturesque village of Rabanal del Camino.

32. Rabanal del Camino to Ponferrada (32 km)

Highlights: The Cruz de Ferro (Iron Cross), and the Templar castle in Ponferrada.

33. Ponferrada to Villafranca del Bierzo (23 km)

Highlights: The vineyards of the Bierzo region and the historic town of Villafranca del Bierzo.

34. Villafranca del Bierzo to O Cebreiro (28 km)

Highlights: The challenging climb to the mountain village of O Cebreiro, known for its Celtic heritage.

35. O Cebreiro to Triacastela (21 km)

Highlights: Beautiful mountain scenery and the village of Triacastela.

36. Triacastela to Sarria (18 km)

Highlights: Scenic paths through forests and the town of Sarria, a popular starting point for the final 100 kilometers.

37. Sarria to Portomarín (22 km)

Highlights: Crossing the medieval bridge into Portomarín, known for its relocated Romanesque church.

38. Portomarín to Palas de Rei (25 km)

Highlights: Rolling hills and scenic paths, the town of Palas de Rei with its medieval heritage.

39. Palas de Rei to Arzúa (29 km)

Highlights: Peaceful woodlands and the cheese-producing town of Arzúa.

40. Arzúa to Pedrouzo (19 km)

Highlights: Quiet rural landscapes, the village of Pedrouzo.

41. Pedrouzo to Santiago de Compostela (20 km)

Highlights: The final stretch to Santiago de Compostela, the emotional arrival at the cathedral, and attending the Pilgrim's Mass.

Key Landmarks and Destinations

1. Seville

Seville Cathedral: The largest Gothic cathedral in the world, housing the tomb of Christopher Columbus. Its Giralda bell tower offers panoramic views of the city.

Alcázar of Seville: A stunning palace complex with beautiful gardens, representing a blend of Islamic and Christian architecture.

Plaza de España: A grand square known for its impressive architecture, ceramic tiles, and picturesque canals.

2. Guillena

Iglesia de Nuestra Señora de Granada: A charming church located in the town center.

3. Castilblanco de los Arroyos

Sierra Norte Natural Park: Nearby natural park offering beautiful landscapes and hiking opportunities.

4. Monesterio

Ham Museum: Showcasing the local tradition of ham production, an important part of the region's culture and economy.

5. Zafra

Plaza Grande and Plaza Chica: Historic squares with beautiful arcades, perfect for enjoying local food and drink.

Alcázar de los Duques de Feria: A historic castle turned into a luxurious parador (hotel).

6. Mérida

Roman Theatre and Amphitheatre: Well-preserved ancient Roman structures hosting performances and tours.

Temple of Diana: An impressive Roman temple situated in the city center.

National Museum of Roman Art: Houses extensive collections of Roman artifacts and mosaics.

7. Cáceres

Old Town (Ciudad Monumental): A UNESCO World Heritage site with medieval walls, towers, and palaces.

Plaza Mayor: The main square surrounded by historic buildings and a great spot for dining.

8. Salamanca

Plaza Mayor: One of the most beautiful squares in Spain, known for its baroque architecture.

University of Salamanca: One of the oldest universities in Europe, with stunning historic buildings and a rich academic heritage.

Cathedral of Salamanca: Featuring both old and new cathedrals, offering a mix of Gothic, Romanesque, and Baroque styles.

9. Zamora

Zamora Cathedral: A Romanesque cathedral with a distinctive Byzantine dome.

Castle of Zamora: Offering panoramic views of the city and the Duero River.

Semana Santa: Zamora is renowned for its Holy Week processions, a deeply rooted religious tradition.

10. Benavente

Castle of the Pimentel: An impressive castle with beautiful views and a rich history.

Church of Santa María del Azogue: A beautiful example of Romanesque architecture.

11. Astorga

Episcopal Palace: Designed by Antoni Gaudí, this modernist building is now a museum dedicated to the Camino de Santiago.

Astorga Cathedral: A stunning Gothic cathedral with a museum showcasing religious art and artifacts.

Roman Ruins: Astorga has several Roman sites, including ancient baths and mosaics.

12. Ponferrada

Templar Castle: A well-preserved fortress built by the Knights Templar, offering tours and historical exhibits.

Basilica de la Encina: Known for its beautiful Renaissance architecture and religious significance.

13. Villafranca del Bierzo

Church of Santiago: Pilgrims who cannot continue to Santiago due to illness can receive the same indulgences here.

Castillo de los Marqueses: A historic castle with beautiful views and gardens.

14. O Cebreiro

Church of Santa María la Real: An ancient pre-Romanesque church with significant religious artifacts.

Pallozas: Traditional round stone houses that offer a glimpse into the past.

15. Santiago de Compostela

Cathedral of Santiago de Compostela: The final destination, featuring the magnificent cathedral where the remains of St. James are believed to be buried. Don't miss the Pilgrim's Mass and the Botafumeiro.

Plaza del Obradoiro: The main square in front of the cathedral, where pilgrims gather to celebrate their arrival.

Museum of Pilgrimage: Offers insights into the history and significance of the Camino.

Natural and Scenic Highlights

Sierra Norte Natural Park: A beautiful natural park near Castilblanco de los Arroyos, offering hiking trails and diverse wildlife.

Roman Bridge of Mérida: Spanning the Guadiana River, this ancient bridge is a testament to Roman engineering and a beautiful spot for photographs.

Ambroz Valley: Known for its stunning autumn colors, this valley offers beautiful landscapes and peaceful walking paths.

Mountains of León: The ascent into the mountains provides breathtaking views and a rewarding challenge for pilgrims.

Galician Countryside: Known for its lush greenery, rolling hills, and picturesque villages. Walking through this region offers a peaceful and scenic experience.

The Via de la Plata is a journey through history, culture, and natural beauty. Each stop along the way provides unique experiences and insights into the rich heritage of Spain. Whether exploring ancient Roman ruins, enjoying the tranquility of rural landscapes, or marveling at architectural wonders, pilgrims on the Via de la Plata are sure to have a memorable and transformative experience.

The Camino Primitivo

The Camino Primitivo, also known as the Original Way, is considered the oldest route of the Camino de Santiago. It stretches approximately 320 kilometers (200 miles) from Oviedo to Santiago de Compostela, passing through the rugged and scenic landscapes of northern Spain. The Camino Primitivo is known for its challenging terrain, historical significance, and stunning natural beauty. Here is an in-depth overview of the Camino Primitivo:

Overview of the Route

Starting Point: Oviedo

Location: The journey begins in the historic city of Oviedo, the capital of the Asturias region.

Highlights: Oviedo is known for its medieval old town, the impressive Cathedral of San Salvador, and its vibrant cultural scene.

Key Stages of the Route

The Camino Primitivo is typically divided into stages, with each stage representing a day's walk. Here are the key stages along the route:

1.Oviedo to Grado (25 km)

Highlights: Leaving the historic city of Oviedo, passing through lush countryside, and arriving in the small town of Grado.

2. Grado to Salas (21 km)

Highlights: Walking through rolling hills, traditional villages, and the charming town of Salas with its medieval tower and castle.

3. Salas to Tineo (20 km)

Highlights: Scenic rural landscapes, forests, and the historic town of Tineo known for its monastery and traditional Asturian architecture.

4. Tineo to Pola de Allande (28 km)

Highlights: Walking through picturesque valleys and small villages, arriving in Pola de Allande with its beautiful church and friendly atmosphere.

5. Pola de Allande to La Mesa (22 km)

Highlights: The challenging ascent to the Puerto del Palo, offering stunning panoramic views, and the descent to the small village of La Mesa.

6. La Mesa to Grandas de Salime (16 km)

Highlights: Scenic mountain paths, the descent to the Grandas de Salime reservoir, and the town of Grandas de Salime with its ethnographic museum.

7. Grandas de Salime to A Fonsagrada (26 km)

Highlights: Crossing into the region of Galicia, walking through forests and rural landscapes, and arriving in the town of A Fonsagrada.

8. A Fonsagrada to O Cádavo (24 km)

Highlights: Walking through traditional Galician villages, rolling hills, and the town of O Cádavo with its historic sites.

9. O Cádavo to Lugo (30 km)

Highlights: Entering the historic city of Lugo, known for its well-preserved Roman walls, beautiful cathedral, and lively old town.

10. Lugo to Ferreira (26 km)

Highlights: Walking through rural Galicia, passing by traditional farms and villages, and arriving in Ferreira.

11. Ferreira to Melide (20 km)

Highlights: Joining the Camino Francés, the town of Melide is famous for its pulpo a la gallega (Galician octopus) and vibrant pilgrim atmosphere.

12. Melide to Arzúa (14 km)

Highlights: Scenic rural paths, forests, and the town of Arzúa known for its cheese and friendly albergues.

13. Arzúa to Pedrouzo (19 km)

Highlights: Quiet rural landscapes, the village of Pedrouzo with its welcoming accommodations and services for pilgrims.

14. Pedrouzo to Santiago de Compostela (20 km)

Highlights: The final stretch to Santiago de Compostela, the emotional arrival at the cathedral, and attending the Pilgrim's Mass.

Key Landmarks and Destinations

Oviedo

Cathedral of San Salvador: A stunning Gothic cathedral housing important relics and known for its connection to the origins of the Camino.

Old Town: Cobblestone streets, historic buildings, and vibrant squares filled with cafes and restaurants.

Grado

Market Square: A lively square with local markets and traditional Asturian architecture.

Church of San Pedro: A beautiful church located in the town center.

Salas

Tower of Valdés-Salas: A medieval tower offering panoramic views of the town and surrounding countryside.

Collegiate Church of Santa María la Mayor: A historic church with a stunning altarpiece.

Tineo

Monastery of Obona: An important pilgrimage site with a rich history.

Church of San Pedro: Known for its beautiful interior and historic significance.

Pola de Allande

Palacio de Cienfuegos: A historic palace offering insights into the region's aristocratic past.

Church of San Andrés: A beautiful example of rural Asturian architecture.

Grandas de Salime

Ethnographic Museum: Showcases traditional Asturian life and culture.

Church of San Salvador: A historic church with beautiful architecture.

Lugo

Roman Walls: A UNESCO World Heritage site, these well-preserved walls encircle the old town and offer a scenic walk.

Lugo Cathedral: A beautiful cathedral with a mix of Romanesque, Gothic, and Baroque styles.

Plaza Mayor: The vibrant main square with cafes, restaurants, and historic buildings.

Melide

Pulperías: Traditional restaurants specializing in pulpo a la gallega (Galician octopus).

Church of San Roque: A historic church known for its beautiful architecture.

Arzúa

Cheese Festival: Known for its delicious local cheese, Arzúa hosts a popular cheese festival.

Church of Santiago: A beautiful church in the heart of Arzúa.

Santiago de Compostela

Cathedral of Santiago de Compostela: The final destination, featuring the magnificent cathedral where the remains of St. James are believed to be buried. Don't miss the Pilgrim's Mass and the Botafumeiro.

Plaza del Obradoiro: The main square in front of the cathedral, where pilgrims gather to celebrate their arrival.

Museum of Pilgrimage: Offers insights into the history and significance of the Camino.

Natural and Scenic Highlights

Puerto del Palo: A challenging mountain pass offering stunning panoramic views of the surrounding landscapes.

Grandas de Salime Reservoir: A beautiful reservoir providing picturesque views and a peaceful walking experience.

Galician Countryside: Known for its lush greenery, rolling hills, and traditional villages. Walking through this region offers a peaceful and scenic experience.

Roman Walls of Lugo: Walking along the top of these ancient walls provides a unique perspective of the historic city and its surroundings.

The Camino Primitivo is a journey through history, culture, and natural beauty. Each stop along the way provides unique experiences and insights into the rich heritage of northern Spain. Whether exploring historic towns, enjoying the tranquility of rural landscapes, or marveling at architectural wonders, pilgrims on the Camino Primitivo are sure to have a memorable and transformative experience.

The Camino Inglés

The Camino Inglés, or the English Way, is a historic route of the Camino de Santiago that dates back to the Middle Ages. It was primarily used by pilgrims from the British Isles and other northern European countries who arrived by sea. The Camino Inglés starts in the port cities of Ferrol or A Coruña in the northwest of Spain and spans approximately 119 kilometers (74 miles) from Ferrol or 74 kilometers (46 miles) from A Coruña to Santiago de Compostela. Here is an in-depth overview of the Camino Inglés:

Overview of the Route

Starting Points: Ferrol and A Coruña

Ferrol: The more popular starting point, known for its naval heritage and beautiful coastline.

A Coruña: An alternative starting point, famous for its historic lighthouse, the Tower of Hercules, and vibrant city life.

Key Stages of the Route

The Camino Inglés is typically divided into stages, with each stage representing a day's walk. Here are the key stages along the route from both starting points:

From Ferrol

1.Ferrol to Neda (14 km)

Highlights: Walking along the scenic coastline, passing by the historic Magdalena neighborhood, and arriving in the charming town of Neda.

2. Neda to Pontedeume (16 km)

Highlights: Crossing the medieval bridge in Neda, walking through picturesque countryside, and reaching the historic town of Pontedeume with its castle and river views.

3. Pontedeume to Betanzos (21 km)

Highlights: Traversing rolling hills and forests, arriving in Betanzos, known for its well-preserved medieval architecture and traditional Galician cuisine.

4. Betanzos to Bruma (28 km)

Highlights: Passing through rural landscapes and small villages, reaching the quiet hamlet of Bruma, offering a peaceful retreat.

5. Bruma to Sigüeiro (24 km)

Highlights: Walking through lush forests and farmland, the village of Sigüeiro provides a welcoming stop with good pilgrim facilities.

6. Sigüeiro to Santiago de Compostela (16 km)

Highlights: The final stretch to Santiago de Compostela, the emotional arrival at the cathedral, and attending the Pilgrim's Mass.

From A Coruña

1.A Coruña to Bruma (33 km)

Highlights: Starting in the vibrant city of A Coruña, passing by the Tower of Hercules, walking through coastal and rural landscapes, and joining the route at Bruma.

2. Bruma to Sigüeiro (24 km)

Highlights: Walking through lush forests and farmland, the village of Sigüeiro provides a welcoming stop with good pilgrim facilities.

3. Sigüeiro to Santiago de Compostela (16 km)

Highlights: The final stretch to Santiago de Compostela, the emotional arrival at the cathedral, and attending the Pilgrim's Mass.

Key Landmarks and Destinations

1.Ferrol

Ferrol Naval Dockyard: One of the most important naval shipyards in Spain with a rich maritime history.

Magdalena District: Known for its grid-pattern streets and beautiful buildings.

San Felipe Castle: Offers stunning views of the estuary and a glimpse into Ferrol's defensive history.

2.Neda

Medieval Bridge: A historic bridge offering picturesque views of the town and river.

Church of Santa María: A charming church located in the town center.

3.Pontedeume

Andrade Tower: A medieval tower offering panoramic views of the town and estuary.

Pontedeume Castle: Historical ruins providing insights into the town's medieval past.

4.Betanzos

San Francisco Church: Known for its beautiful Gothic architecture and historic significance.

Praza dos Irmáns García Naveira: A lively square surrounded by historic buildings and cafes.

5.Bruma

Chapel of San Lorenzo: A small chapel providing a peaceful retreat for pilgrims.

6.Sigüeiro

River Tambre: Offers scenic views and a peaceful walking path along the river.

Church of San Andrés: A historic church in the village center.

7.A Coruña

Tower of Hercules: The oldest functioning Roman lighthouse in the world and a UNESCO World Heritage site.

Maria Pita Square: The main square named after the local heroine Maria Pita, surrounded by beautiful buildings and cafes.

Riazor Beach: A popular beach offering a great place to relax and enjoy the ocean views.

8.Santiago de Compostela

Cathedral of Santiago de Compostela: The final destination, featuring the magnificent cathedral where the remains of St. James are believed to be buried. Don't miss the Pilgrim's Mass and the Botafumeiro.

Plaza del Obradoiro: The main square in front of the cathedral, where pilgrims gather to celebrate their arrival.

Museum of Pilgrimage: Offers insights into the history and significance of the Camino.

Natural and Scenic Highlights

Ferrol Estuary: Walking along the estuary provides beautiful coastal views and a peaceful start to the journey.

Rural Galicia: The route passes through lush forests, rolling hills, and traditional Galician villages, offering a serene and picturesque walking experience.

Coastal Views from A Coruña: Starting in A Coruña offers beautiful coastal views, including the iconic Tower of Hercules and the beaches along the Atlantic Ocean.

Forests and Farmland: The path from Bruma to Santiago de Compostela is characterized by lush green forests and scenic farmland, providing a tranquil environment for reflection and walking.

Cultural Insights

Galician Culture: Throughout the route, pilgrims can experience the unique culture of Galicia, including its language (Galician), traditional music, and festivals.

Cuisine: The Camino Inglés offers opportunities to enjoy traditional Galician cuisine, including fresh seafood, empanadas, pulpo a la gallega (Galician octopus), and the famous Tarta de Santiago (almond cake).

Historic Towns and Villages: Each stop along the way offers insights into the rich history and architecture of the region, from medieval bridges and churches to historic squares and castles.

The Camino Inglés is a journey through history, culture, and natural beauty. Each stop along the way provides unique experiences and insights into the rich heritage of northern Spain. Whether exploring historic towns, enjoying the tranquility of rural landscapes, or marveling at architectural wonders, pilgrims on the Camino Inglés are sure to have a memorable and transformative experience.

Unique Experiences on Less Traveled Paths

The lesser-known routes of the Camino de Santiago, such as the Via de la Plata, Camino Primitivo, and Camino Inglés, offer unique and enriching experiences that differ from the more popular routes like the Camino Francés. Here are some of the distinctive experiences you can enjoy on these less traveled paths:

The Via de la Plata

1. Historical Insights:

Roman Heritage: The Via de la Plata follows an ancient Roman road, and along the way, you can explore numerous Roman ruins, including bridges, aqueducts, and theatres. Mérida, in particular, is renowned for its well-preserved Roman monuments.

Medieval Towns: Discover charming medieval towns such as Zafra, with its Moorish influences and historic architecture.

2. Cultural Immersion:

Local Festivals: Experience traditional Spanish festivals, such as Semana Santa (Holy Week) in Zamora, which features solemn processions and centuries-old traditions.

Gastronomy: Enjoy regional delicacies, including Extremadura's famous jamón ibérico (Iberian ham), and sample local wines and cheeses along the way.

3. Natural Beauty:

Diverse Landscapes: The route traverses a variety of landscapes, from the rolling plains of Extremadura to the lush greenery of Galicia. The Ambroz Valley, particularly in autumn, offers stunning scenery with vibrant fall colors.

Wildlife: Spot native wildlife in the Sierra Norte Natural Park and other natural reserves along the route.

4. Solitude and Reflection:

Less Crowded: The Via de la Plata is less frequented than other Camino routes, offering a quieter, more introspective journey. Pilgrims often find it easier to connect with nature and experience moments of solitude and reflection.

The Camino Primitivo

1. Historical Significance:

Ancient Route: The Camino Primitivo is considered the oldest Camino route, first traveled by King Alfonso II in the 9th century. Walking this path connects you with the earliest pilgrims' footsteps.

Medieval Architecture: Explore well-preserved medieval structures, such as the Roman walls of Lugo, which provide a glimpse into the past.

2. Cultural Encounters:

Asturian Culture: Immerse yourself in the unique culture of Asturias, known for its traditional music, dance, and cider production. Visit local sidrerías (cider houses) to experience the distinctive way cider is poured and enjoyed.

Galician Traditions: In Galicia, enjoy local festivals and traditional foods, such as empanadas and pulpo a la gallega (Galician octopus).

3. Scenic and Challenging Terrain:

Mountain Passes: The route's challenging terrain includes mountain passes like the Puerto del Palo, offering breathtaking panoramic views and a sense of accomplishment upon reaching the summits.

Rural Landscapes: The Camino Primitivo winds through remote rural areas, with lush forests, rolling hills, and peaceful valleys providing a tranquil and scenic walking experience.

4. Unique Accommodations:

Historic Albergues: Stay in historic albergues and monasteries, such as the Monastery of San Salvador in Grandas de Salime, which offer a unique and spiritual overnight experience.

The Camino Inglés

1. Maritime Heritage:

Port Cities: Starting from the historic port cities of Ferrol or A Coruña, you can explore their rich maritime heritage. Visit naval museums, historic shipyards, and the iconic Tower of Hercules in A Coruña.

Coastal Views: Enjoy stunning coastal views as you walk along the coastline, with opportunities to relax on beautiful beaches and enjoy the fresh sea air.

2. Historical Pilgrimage:

Ancient Path: Follow the footsteps of medieval pilgrims who traveled from northern Europe to Santiago de Compostela. The route is steeped in history and tradition.

Historic Churches: Visit ancient churches and chapels along the way, such as the Church of San Francisco in Betanzos, which dates back to the 14th century.

3. Culinary Delights:

Galician Cuisine: Savor the flavors of Galicia with fresh seafood, traditional empanadas, and the famous Tarta de Santiago (almond cake). The towns along the route offer excellent dining options.

Local Markets: Explore local markets where you can buy fresh produce, artisanal cheeses, and other local specialties.

4. Intimate Pilgrimage Experience:

Small Villages: The Camino Inglés passes through charming small villages and rural areas, allowing for intimate encounters with local residents and fellow pilgrims.

Quiet Reflection: With fewer pilgrims on this route, you can enjoy moments of quiet reflection and personal contemplation, making it a deeply spiritual journey.

General Tips for Lesser-Known Routes

1. Preparation:

Training: Prepare physically for the challenging terrain of these routes. Regular walking, especially on varied terrain, will help build stamina and strength.

Gear: Ensure you have high-quality, comfortable footwear and pack appropriately for the varying weather conditions you may encounter.

2. Navigation:

Maps and Guides: Carry reliable maps and guidebooks specific to your chosen route. Digital apps can also be useful for navigation and finding accommodations.

Waymarking: While these routes are generally well-marked, pay attention to waymarkers and be aware of potential detours or alternative paths.

3. Accommodation:

Advance Booking: In smaller villages, accommodation options may be limited. Consider booking in advance, especially during peak pilgrimage seasons.

Local Albergues: Support local albergues and guesthouses, which often provide a more personal and culturally immersive experience.

4. Connecting with Fellow Pilgrims:

Community: Even on less traveled routes, the sense of community among pilgrims is strong. Take the opportunity to share stories and experiences with fellow travelers.

Language: Learning a few basic phrases in Spanish (and Galician in Galicia) can enhance your interactions with locals and fellow pilgrims.

Embarking on one of these lesser-known Camino routes offers a unique and enriching pilgrimage experience. From historical insights and cultural encounters to stunning natural landscapes and moments of quiet reflection, these paths provide an opportunity to explore a different side of the Camino de Santiago.

Chapter 7
Daily Life on the Camino

Pilgrim Etiquette and Traditions

Walking the Camino de Santiago is not only a physical journey but also a deeply spiritual and communal experience. Understanding and respecting the etiquette and traditions of the Camino can enhance your pilgrimage and help you connect with fellow pilgrims and the local communities you encounter along the way. Here are some key aspects of pilgrim etiquette and traditions:

Pilgrim Etiquette

1. Respectful Behavior:

Quiet in Albergues: Albergues are shared spaces where pilgrims rest and recover. Maintain silence or speak softly, especially during the designated quiet hours (typically between 10 PM and 6 AM).

Cleanliness: Keep your sleeping area tidy and clean up after yourself in common areas, including kitchens and bathrooms. Dispose of trash properly and leave the place as you found it.

Lights and Noise: Use a headlamp or flashlight if you need to move around after lights-out. Avoid rustling plastic bags or making noise that could disturb others.

2. Sharing Space:

Bunk Beds: If using a top bunk, be considerate when climbing up or down. Avoid placing your belongings on someone else's bed.

Bathrooms and Showers: Be mindful of time spent in shared bathrooms and showers. Leave the facilities clean for the next person.

3. Greeting Fellow Pilgrims:

Buen Camino: This traditional greeting, meaning "Good Way," is exchanged among pilgrims. It fosters a sense of camaraderie and shared purpose.

Politeness: Greet locals and fellow pilgrims with a smile and polite conversation. Simple courtesies go a long way in building positive interactions.

4. Walking Etiquette:

Single File: Walk in single file on narrow paths to allow others to pass. On wider paths, walk side by side but be aware of your surroundings.

Yielding: Yield to faster walkers and cyclists by stepping aside. On steep descents, yield to those coming uphill.

Stay on the Path: Stick to the marked path to avoid damaging crops or private property. Respect the natural environment and local communities.

5. Pilgrim Passport (Credencial):

Stamps: Collect stamps (sellos) at albergues, churches, and other points along the way. These stamps are proof of your journey and are required to receive the Compostela in Santiago.

Respect for Sites: When visiting churches and other sacred sites, behave respectfully. Dress modestly and observe any specific guidelines provided.

6. Supporting Local Economy:

Local Businesses: Support local businesses by purchasing meals, drinks, and supplies from local shops and restaurants. This helps sustain the communities along the Camino.

Donations: Many albergues are donation-based (donativo). Contribute what you can to help maintain these facilities for future pilgrims.

Pilgrim Traditions

1. Pilgrim Blessing:

Cathedral of San Salvador in Oviedo: Many pilgrims start their journey with a blessing at the Cathedral of San Salvador. This tradition dates back to the early days of the Camino.

Blessings in Churches: Throughout the Camino, churches often offer blessings for pilgrims. Participating in these ceremonies can be a meaningful part of your journey.

2. Leaving Stones at Cruz de Ferro:

Symbolic Act: At the Cruz de Ferro (Iron Cross) on the Camino Francés, pilgrims leave a stone or token brought from home. This symbolizes leaving behind burdens and making a fresh start.

3. Pilgrim Shell (Concha):

Symbol of the Camino: The scallop shell is a symbol of the Camino de Santiago. Pilgrims often attach a shell to their backpacks. It serves as a badge of honor and a sign of their journey.

Historical Significance: Historically, the shell was proof that a pilgrim had reached Santiago. It also served practical purposes, such as scooping water.

4. Pilgrim's Staff (Bordón):

Traditional Gear: The pilgrim's staff, or bordón, is a traditional walking stick used for support and protection. It is a symbol of the pilgrim's journey and a practical tool for walking.

5. Attending Pilgrim Mass:

Pilgrim Mass: Many churches along the Camino offer special pilgrim masses. The Pilgrim's Mass in the Cathedral of Santiago is a highlight, featuring the famous Botafumeiro (incense thurible) on special occasions.

Community Gathering: Attending mass is an opportunity to gather with fellow pilgrims, reflect on your journey, and give thanks.

6. Writing in Pilgrim Books:

Guest Books: Many albergues and churches have guest books where pilgrims can leave messages, reflections, and well-wishes. Writing in these books connects you with the larger pilgrim community.

7. Compostela Certificate:

Completion Certificate: Upon reaching Santiago, pilgrims can receive the Compostela, a certificate of completion. It is awarded to those who have walked at least the last 100 kilometers (62 miles) or cycled the last 200 kilometers (124 miles) to Santiago.

Pilgrim's Office: Visit the Pilgrim's Office in Santiago to present your stamped credencial and receive the Compostela.

Tips for a Respectful Pilgrimage

1. Personal Reflection:

Mindfulness: Use the journey for personal reflection and mindfulness. Embrace the opportunity for spiritual growth and self-discovery.

Journaling: Keep a journal of your experiences, thoughts, and emotions. It can be a valuable tool for reflection and remembrance.

2. Helping Others:

Support Fellow Pilgrims: Offer help and encouragement to fellow pilgrims, whether it's sharing food, offering a kind word, or helping with directions.

Volunteer Opportunities: Consider volunteering at albergues or pilgrim support organizations to give back to the Camino community.

3. Environmental Stewardship:

Leave No Trace: Follow the principles of Leave No Trace by minimizing your environmental impact. Carry out all trash, avoid disturbing wildlife, and respect natural habitats.

Sustainable Practices: Use reusable water bottles and bags, and support eco-friendly businesses along the route.

By adhering to these guidelines and embracing the traditions of the Camino, you can ensure a respectful and enriching pilgrimage experience. The Camino de Santiago is not just a physical journey but also a spiritual and communal one. Respecting the etiquette and traditions helps maintain the spirit of the Camino and fosters a sense of connection among pilgrims and the local communities.

Managing Finances and Budgeting

Walking the Camino de Santiago is a rewarding experience, but it requires careful planning and budgeting to ensure you can enjoy your journey without financial stress. Here are some tips and guidelines for managing your finances and budgeting effectively while on the Camino:

Budgeting Basics

1. Estimating Costs:

Accommodation: The cost of accommodation can vary widely. Albergues (pilgrim hostels) typically cost between €5 and €15 per night. Private rooms or hotels can range from €25 to €100 per night, depending on the level of comfort and location.

Food and Drink: Daily food expenses can range from €20 to €30. This includes pilgrim menus (Menú del Peregrino) which usually cost between €10 and €15, breakfast, snacks, and drinks.

Miscellaneous Expenses: Include budget for laundry, personal items, and any sightseeing or additional activities. This can add another €5 to €10 per day.

2. Setting a Daily Budget:

Basic Pilgrim Budget: For those staying in albergues and eating pilgrim menus, a daily budget of €30 to €40 is reasonable.

Comfortable Budget: For those preferring private rooms or hotels and occasional restaurant meals, a daily budget of €50 to €70 is more appropriate.

Luxury Budget: If you prefer high-end accommodations and dining, budget upwards of €100 per day.

Cost-Saving Tips

1. Accommodation:

Municipal and Parish Albergues: These are often the cheapest options. They are sometimes donativo (donation-based), meaning you pay what you can afford.

Private Albergues: Slightly more expensive but often offer more amenities, such as private rooms and better facilities.

Camping: In some areas, camping is an option. This can be very cost-effective but requires carrying additional gear.

2. Food and Drink:

Cook Your Own Meals: Many albergues have kitchens where you can prepare your own food. Buying groceries and cooking can significantly reduce food costs.

Picnic Lunches: Purchase bread, cheese, fruits, and other snacks from local markets for a cost-effective and enjoyable picnic lunch.

Tapas and Pintxos: In regions like Galicia and the Basque Country, you can enjoy affordable and delicious tapas and pintxos at local bars.

3. Transport:

Public Transport: Use buses or trains for any long-distance travel to or from the Camino. These are usually more cost-effective than taxis.

Walking: Stick to walking as much as possible. It's free and part of the pilgrimage experience.

4. Gear and Supplies:

Buy Quality Gear: Invest in good-quality, durable gear that will last the entire journey, reducing the need for replacements.

Second-Hand Stores: Consider purchasing gear from second-hand stores or borrowing items from friends or family.

Managing Money

1. Currency and Payments:

Euro (€): Spain uses the Euro. Ensure you have enough cash for small purchases, as some smaller towns and albergues may not accept credit cards.

ATMs: ATMs are available in most towns and cities along the Camino. Plan to withdraw larger amounts to minimize transaction fees, but be mindful of safety when carrying cash.

Credit/Debit Cards: Widely accepted in larger establishments, but always have cash as a backup.

2. Avoiding Extra Fees:

Foreign Transaction Fees: Check with your bank about foreign transaction fees and consider using a card that offers fee-free international transactions.

ATM Fees: Be aware of potential ATM fees and consider withdrawing larger amounts less frequently to minimize these charges.

Emergency Fund

1. Setting Aside Funds:

Unexpected Expenses: Set aside an emergency fund of at least €200 to cover unexpected expenses, such as medical emergencies, transportation changes, or gear replacement.

Accessible Funds: Keep this money easily accessible but separate from your daily spending cash to avoid dipping into it unnecessarily.

2. Travel Insurance:

Coverage: Consider purchasing travel insurance that covers medical expenses, trip cancellations, and lost or stolen items. This can provide peace of mind and financial protection.

Documentation: Carry copies of your insurance policy and emergency contact numbers.

Tips for Sticking to Your Budget

1. Track Your Spending:

Daily Log: Keep a daily log of your expenses to monitor your spending and ensure you stay within your budget.

Apps: Use budgeting apps to help track expenses and manage your budget more efficiently.

2. Plan Ahead:

Daily Itinerary: Plan your daily itinerary, including where you will stay and eat, to avoid last-minute decisions that could lead to overspending.

Rest Days: Plan rest days in towns with affordable accommodation and amenities.

3. Prioritize Spending:

Needs vs. Wants: Focus on essential expenses such as accommodation, food, and transportation. Limit spending on non-essentials like souvenirs or expensive meals.

Shared Costs: Share costs with fellow pilgrims for things like accommodation, groceries, and transportation.

4. Be Flexible:

Adjust Plans: Be prepared to adjust your plans if you find you are overspending. Opt for cheaper accommodation or dining options if needed.

Unexpected Savings: Take advantage of unexpected savings opportunities, such as free meals offered by albergues or discounted rates for pilgrims.

By carefully planning and managing your finances, you can ensure a stress-free and enjoyable pilgrimage on the Camino de Santiago. Following these tips will help you stay within your budget and make the most of your journey.

Navigating Language Barriers

Walking the Camino de Santiago is an enriching experience that often involves interacting with locals and fellow pilgrims from various countries. While Spanish is the primary language spoken along the Camino, and Galician in Galicia, you will encounter many other languages spoken by international pilgrims. Here are some tips and strategies for effectively navigating language barriers on your pilgrimage:

Basic Spanish Phrases

Learning a few basic Spanish phrases can significantly enhance your Camino experience. Here are some essential phrases to get you started:

Greetings:

Hola (Hello)

Buenos días (Good morning)

Buenas tardes (Good afternoon)

Buenas noches (Good evening/night)

Adiós (Goodbye)

Common Expressions:

Por favor (Please)

Gracias (Thank you)

De nada (You're welcome)

Perdón/Disculpe (Excuse me/Sorry)

Sí (Yes)

No (No)

Questions:

¿Cómo está? (How are you?)

¿Dónde está...? (Where is...?)

¿Cuánto cuesta? (How much does it cost?)

¿Habla inglés? (Do you speak English?)

¿Puede ayudarme? (Can you help me?)

Camino-Specific:

Buen Camino (Good Way)

¿Dónde está el albergue? (Where is the hostel?)

Necesito una cama, por favor (I need a bed, please)

¿A qué hora es la misa del peregrino? (What time is the pilgrim mass?)

¿Dónde puedo sellar mi credencial? (Where can I get my credential stamped?)

Language Resources

1. Phrasebooks:

Carry a Phrasebook: A compact Spanish phrasebook can be a valuable resource for quick reference. Look for one that includes Camino-specific vocabulary.

2. Language Apps:

Translation Apps: Use apps like Google Translate, Duolingo, or Babbel to help with translations and learning basic phrases. Google Translate also offers a camera function to translate signs and menus.

Offline Mode: Download the offline language packs for your apps to ensure you have access to translations even without internet connectivity.

3. Camino Apps:

Camino-Specific Apps: Some apps are designed specifically for the Camino de Santiago and include useful phrases, maps, and information on albergues.

Communication Strategies

1. Non-Verbal Communication:

Gestures: Use universal gestures, such as pointing, nodding, and shaking your head, to convey basic messages.

Facial Expressions: Smile, maintain eye contact, and use facial expressions to show friendliness and understanding.

2. Writing and Drawing:

Notepad: Carry a small notepad and pen to write down questions or draw simple pictures if verbal communication fails.

Phone: Use your phone to show written phrases or translations.

3. Simplify Your Language:

Speak Slowly: Speak slowly and clearly, using simple words and short sentences.

Avoid Idioms: Avoid idiomatic expressions and slang that may not be understood.

4. Ask for Help:

Locals and Fellow Pilgrims: Don't hesitate to ask for help from locals or fellow pilgrims who may speak both Spanish and your language. Many people are happy to assist.

Cultural Sensitivity

1. Respect Local Customs:

Politeness: Always be polite and show respect for local customs and traditions. A little courtesy goes a long way.

Dress Appropriately: In churches and religious sites, dress modestly and follow any specific guidelines.

2. Learn About Regional Languages:

Galician: In Galicia, Galician (Galego) is commonly spoken alongside Spanish. Learning a few Galician phrases can be appreciated by locals.

Galician Phrases:

Bos días (Good morning)

Grazas (Thank you)

Por favor (Please)

Onde está...? (Where is...?)

3. Be Patient and Positive:

Patience: Be patient with yourself and others when facing language barriers. Misunderstandings can happen, but staying calm and positive helps resolve them.

Positivity: Approach language challenges with a sense of humor and openness. They are part of the adventure and learning experience.

Engaging with the Community

1. Attend Pilgrim Masses and Events:

Pilgrim Masses: Attend pilgrim masses and local events to immerse yourself in the culture and practice your language skills.

Social Gatherings: Join communal meals or gatherings in albergues to interact with fellow pilgrims and locals.

2. Volunteer Opportunities:

Volunteer: Consider volunteering at albergues or pilgrim support organizations. It's a great way to give back and improve your language skills through practice.

Useful Tools

1. Language Learning Tools:

Duolingo: Offers a fun and interactive way to learn basic Spanish and Galician.

Babbel: Provides structured lessons that are great for beginners.

Rosetta Stone: A comprehensive language learning tool for in-depth study.

2. Communication Devices:

Pocket Translators: Electronic pocket translators can quickly translate spoken and written phrases.

Smartphones: Use your smartphone with downloaded language apps for quick and easy translations.

Navigating language barriers on the Camino de Santiago can enhance your experience, offering opportunities to learn, connect, and grow. By preparing with basic phrases, using helpful tools, and embracing the adventure, you can communicate effectively and make the most of your pilgrimage.

Dealing with Challenges and Staying Motivated

Walking the Camino de Santiago is a rewarding but demanding journey that presents various physical, mental, and emotional challenges. Staying motivated and overcoming these obstacles is crucial for a successful pilgrimage. Here are some tips and strategies to help you deal with challenges and maintain motivation on the Camino:

Physical Challenges

1. Blisters and Foot Pain:

Proper Footwear: Ensure you have well-fitting, broken-in hiking boots or shoes. Invest in high-quality, moisture-wicking socks.

Foot Care: Regularly check your feet for hot spots and treat them immediately to prevent blisters. Use blister prevention products like moleskin, blister pads, or Vaseline.

Rest and Air Out: Take breaks to rest your feet and air them out. Remove your shoes and socks during longer breaks to let your feet breathe.

2. Muscle Fatigue and Soreness:

Stretching: Perform regular stretching exercises before and after walking to maintain flexibility and prevent muscle stiffness.

Hydration: Stay hydrated to help reduce muscle cramps and fatigue. Drink plenty of water throughout the day.

Nutrition: Eat a balanced diet with sufficient protein and carbohydrates to fuel your body and aid muscle recovery.

3. Heavy Backpack:

Pack Light: Only bring essential items and keep your backpack weight to a minimum. Aim for no more than 10% of your body weight.

Adjust Fit: Ensure your backpack fits properly and adjust the straps to distribute the weight evenly.

4. Weather Conditions:

Rain Gear: Carry a waterproof jacket, pants, and a cover for your backpack to stay dry in wet weather.

Sun Protection: Use sunscreen, wear a hat, and carry sunglasses to protect yourself from the sun.

Layering: Dress in layers to adjust to changing temperatures throughout the day.

Mental and Emotional Challenges

1. Homesickness and Loneliness:

Stay Connected: Keep in touch with family and friends through phone calls, messages, or social media. Sharing your journey can provide emotional support.

Fellow Pilgrims: Build connections with fellow pilgrims. Sharing stories and experiences can help alleviate feelings of loneliness.

2. Mental Fatigue:

Mindfulness and Meditation: Practice mindfulness or meditation to stay present and focused. Take time each day to reflect and relax.

Positive Thinking: Focus on positive aspects of your journey and celebrate small achievements. Reframe negative thoughts and remind yourself of your purpose.

3. Motivation:

Set Goals: Set daily and overall goals for your pilgrimage. Having clear objectives can provide motivation and a sense of accomplishment.

Mantras and Affirmations: Use personal mantras or affirmations to boost your morale and keep you focused on your journey.

Visualize Completion: Imagine reaching Santiago de Compostela and the sense of achievement you will feel. Visualization can be a powerful motivational tool.

Practical Strategies

1. Daily Routine:

Consistent Schedule: Establish a daily routine to create structure. Start your day early to take advantage of cooler temperatures and quieter paths.

Regular Breaks: Take regular breaks to rest, hydrate, and refuel. Short, frequent breaks can prevent exhaustion and maintain energy levels.

2. Plan Ahead:

Itinerary: Plan your daily stages but remain flexible to adjust based on your condition and circumstances.

Rest Days: Schedule rest days to recover and explore the local area. Rest days can prevent burnout and rejuvenate your body and mind.

3. Stay Informed:

Weather Updates: Check weather forecasts to prepare for the day's conditions.

Local Information: Stay informed about local services, accommodation options, and any route changes.

Community Support

1. Pilgrim Network:

Supportive Community: Engage with the Camino community. Pilgrims often support each other, share tips, and offer encouragement.

Online Groups: Join online Camino forums or social media groups for advice, support, and camaraderie.

2. Local Assistance:

Albergue Hosts: Albergue hosts can provide valuable information and assistance. Don't hesitate to ask for help or recommendations.

Local Residents: Interacting with local residents can offer insights and enhance your experience. Many locals are friendly and supportive of pilgrims.

Inspirational Sources

1. Pilgrim Stories:

Books and Documentaries: Read books or watch documentaries about the Camino to draw inspiration from others' experiences.

Pilgrim Stories: Share and listen to stories from fellow pilgrims. Hearing about others' journeys can provide motivation and perspective.

2. Personal Reflection:

Journal Writing: Keep a journal to document your thoughts, challenges, and achievements. Writing can be therapeutic and help you process your experiences.

Gratitude Practice: Practice gratitude by noting things you are thankful for each day. Focusing on positive aspects can boost your mood and motivation.

Dealing with Unexpected Challenges

1. Flexibility and Adaptability:

Stay Flexible: Be prepared to adapt your plans if necessary. Flexibility can help you navigate unexpected challenges more smoothly.

Problem-Solving: Approach challenges with a problem-solving mindset. Break down the issue and consider possible solutions.

2. Health and Safety:

Medical Kit: Carry a basic medical kit for minor injuries and ailments. Know the location of medical facilities along your route.

Safety First: Prioritize your safety. If you feel unwell or face difficult conditions, don't hesitate to seek help or rest.

Chapter 8

Cultural and Historical Highlights

Historical Sites Along the Way

Walking the Camino de Santiago offers not only a spiritual journey but also a rich cultural and historical experience. The route is dotted with numerous historical sites that reflect the deep heritage and traditions of the regions it traverses. Here are some of the most significant historical sites you will encounter along the way:

1. St. Jean Pied de Port

Citadel and Old Town: The starting point for many pilgrims on the Camino Francés, St. Jean Pied de Port boasts a charming old town and a citadel that dates back to the 17th century.

2. Roncesvalles

Collegiate Church of Santa María: This 13th-century Gothic church is an important stop for pilgrims, offering a moment of reflection and a glimpse into the medieval past.

3. Pamplona

Pamplona Cathedral: A stunning Gothic cathedral with a beautiful cloister and an impressive collection of religious artifacts.

Plaza del Castillo: The heart of the city, surrounded by historic buildings and vibrant cafes.

4. Puente la Reina

Romanesque Bridge: This iconic bridge, built in the 11th century, is a marvel of medieval engineering and a significant landmark on the Camino.

5. Estella

Palacio de los Reyes de Navarra: A 12th-century Romanesque palace, one of the few civil buildings from that period in Spain.

Church of San Pedro de la Rúa: Known for its beautiful cloister and Romanesque architecture.

6. Logroño

Santa María de la Redonda Cathedral: Features two stunning baroque towers and an impressive collection of religious art.

Puente de Piedra: An important bridge over the Ebro River, dating back to the 12th century.

7. Burgos

Burgos Cathedral: A UNESCO World Heritage site, this Gothic cathedral is renowned for its stunning architecture and intricate details.

Monastery of Santa María la Real de Las Huelgas: A historic monastery founded in the 12th century with significant religious and historical importance.

8. Frómista

Church of San Martín: A perfectly preserved example of Romanesque architecture, dating back to the 11th century.

9. León

León Cathedral: Famous for its impressive stained glass windows, this Gothic cathedral is a highlight of the Camino.

Basilica of San Isidoro: Known as the "Sistine Chapel of Romanesque Art" for its beautiful frescoes.

10. Astorga

Episcopal Palace: Designed by Antoni Gaudí, this modernist building now houses the Camino Museum.

Astorga Cathedral: An impressive Gothic cathedral with elements of Baroque and Renaissance styles.

11. Ponferrada

Templar Castle: A well-preserved fortress built by the Knights Templar in the 12th century, offering panoramic views of the city.

12. O Cebreiro

Santa María la Real Church: A pre-Romanesque church that houses the Holy Grail of Galicia, an important religious relic.

Pallozas: Traditional thatched stone houses that provide a glimpse into the region's Celtic past.

13. Samos

Monastery of San Xulián de Samos: One of the oldest monasteries in Spain, dating back to the 6th century, with beautiful cloisters and a rich history.

14. Portomarín

Church of San Nicolás: A Romanesque church that was moved stone-by-stone to its current location when the village was flooded to create a reservoir.

15. Santiago de Compostela

Cathedral of Santiago de Compostela: The final destination of the Camino, this magnificent cathedral houses the relics of St. James and is a UNESCO World Heritage site.

Plaza del Obradoiro: The grand square in front of the cathedral, where pilgrims gather to celebrate their journey's end.

Tips for Visiting Historical Sites

1. Respect the Sites: Many of these historical sites are still active places of worship. Be respectful of local customs and traditions, and maintain a quiet and reverent demeanor.

2. Guided Tours: Consider joining guided tours at major sites to gain deeper insights into their historical and cultural significance.

3. Photography: While photography is usually allowed, always check for any restrictions, especially in places of worship.

4. Local Cuisine: Many historical towns along the Camino offer unique local dishes. Take the opportunity to try regional specialties and immerse yourself in the local culture.

5. Souvenirs: Purchase souvenirs from local artisans to support the communities and keep a memento of your journey.

The Camino de Santiago is not only a physical journey but also a voyage through history. Each historical site along the way adds depth to your pilgrimage, connecting you with the rich tapestry of the past and enhancing your overall experience.

Local Festivals and Events

Experiencing local festivals and events along the Camino de Santiago can add a vibrant and enriching dimension to your pilgrimage. These celebrations offer insights into the region's cultural heritage, traditions, and community spirit. Here are some of the notable festivals and events you may encounter along the Camino:

1. Fiesta de San Fermín (Pamplona)

When: July 6-14

Highlights: Known worldwide for the running of the bulls, this festival also features parades, music, fireworks, and traditional dances. It's a thrilling and culturally rich event that showcases the spirit of Pamplona.

2. Fiesta de Santiago (Santiago de Compostela)

When: July 25

Highlights: This festival honors Saint James, the patron saint of Spain. Celebrations include religious ceremonies, parades, traditional music, and dance performances. The festivities culminate in a spectacular fireworks display at the Plaza del Obradoiro.

3. Semana Santa (Various Locations)

When: Holy Week, leading up to Easter Sunday

Highlights: Semana Santa, or Holy Week, features solemn processions, elaborate floats, and religious ceremonies. Cities like León, Burgos, and Logroño have particularly impressive celebrations.

4. Feria de Abril (Seville)

When: Two weeks after Easter

Highlights: Although not directly on the Camino, the Feria de Abril in Seville is worth visiting if you're in Spain during this time. The festival includes flamenco dancing, bullfighting, horse parades, and vibrant fairgrounds with food and drink.

5. Batalla del Vino (Haro)

When: June 29

Highlights: In the town of Haro in La Rioja, this unique festival involves a massive wine fight where participants drench each other in red wine. It's a fun and lively event that celebrates the region's rich winemaking heritage.

6. La Rioja Wine Harvest Festival (Logroño)

When: Late September

Highlights: This festival celebrates the grape harvest with wine tastings, parades, traditional music, and dances. It's an excellent opportunity to sample some of the best wines from the famous Rioja region.

7. Festival Internacional de Teatro de Calle (Lugo)

When: July

Highlights: This international street theater festival in Lugo features performances by artists from around the world. The city's historic streets come alive with drama, comedy, and acrobatics.

8. Corpus Christi (Various Locations)

When: June (60 days after Easter Sunday)

Highlights: Corpus Christi is celebrated with elaborate processions, flower carpets, and religious ceremonies.

Cities like Toledo and Pontevedra have particularly notable celebrations.

9. San Juan Festival (La Coruña)

When: June 23-24

Highlights: This festival celebrates the summer solstice with bonfires, fireworks, and beach parties. It's a magical night filled with music, dancing, and a strong sense of community.

10. Mercado Medieval (Various Locations)

When: Throughout the year

Highlights: Many towns along the Camino host medieval markets featuring artisans, traditional crafts, music, and food. These markets transport you back in time and offer a unique cultural experience.

Tips for Enjoying Local Festivals

1. Plan Ahead: Research festival dates and plan your route to coincide with these events. Accommodations can fill up quickly, so book early if you plan to stay overnight.

2. Participate: Engage with the festivities by joining in the dances, tasting local foods, and learning about the traditions. It's a great way to connect with locals and fellow pilgrims.

3. Respect Traditions: Understand the cultural significance of the festivals and show respect for the local customs and religious practices.

4. Stay Safe: Festivals can be crowded and lively. Keep an eye on your belongings and stay aware of your surroundings.

5. Capture Memories: Bring a camera to capture the vibrant colors, lively performances, and joyful moments. These memories will be a treasured part of your Camino experience.

Personal Experiences

1. Engaging with Locals: Participating in festivals allowed me to connect with the local community and experience their warmth and hospitality. Sharing a meal or dance with locals made the journey even more special.

2. Unique Traditions: Witnessing unique traditions, such as the wine fight in Haro or the solemn processions of Semana Santa, provided a deeper understanding of the cultural diversity and history along the Camino.

3. Memorable Moments: From the fireworks at the Fiesta de Santiago to the lively music at the Feria de

Abril, these festivals created unforgettable memories that enriched my pilgrimage.

Local festivals and events along the Camino de Santiago offer a glimpse into the vibrant cultural tapestry of Spain. They provide opportunities to celebrate, reflect, and connect with the rich traditions that have shaped the Camino over centuries. Embrace these experiences as part of your journey, and let them add color and joy to your pilgrimage.

Regional Cuisine and Culinary Delights

One of the most enjoyable aspects of walking the Camino de Santiago is sampling the diverse and delicious regional cuisines. Each region you pass through offers unique dishes and culinary traditions that reflect its local culture and history. Here are some regional culinary highlights you won't want to miss:

1. Navarra

Chistorra: A type of fresh, short sausage made with minced pork and seasoned with garlic and paprika. Often grilled or fried, it's a local favorite.

Pimientos del Piquillo: Small, sweet red peppers, usually roasted and stuffed with various fillings such as meat, seafood, or cheese.

Estofado de Toro: A hearty bull stew, reflecting the region's tradition of bullfighting.

2. La Rioja

Rioja Wine: World-renowned for its red wines, a visit to La Rioja is incomplete without sampling its rich, robust wines.

Patatas a la Riojana: A traditional potato stew with chorizo, garlic, and paprika, perfect for a pilgrim's meal.

Chuletas al Sarmiento: Lamb chops grilled over vine cuttings, offering a smoky and flavorful taste.

3. Castilla y León

Cochinillo Asado: Roast suckling pig, particularly famous in Segovia. It's tender and flavorful with crispy skin.

Lechazo Asado: Roast lamb, another regional specialty, often prepared in wood-fired ovens.

Morcilla de Burgos: A type of blood sausage made with rice, onions, and spices, typically grilled or fried.

4. Galicia

Pulpo a la Gallega: Octopus served with olive oil, paprika, and salt, often enjoyed with potatoes. It's a must-try dish in Galicia.

Empanada Gallega: A large pie filled with meat, fish, or vegetables, wrapped in a thick, bread-like dough.

Tarta de Santiago: A traditional almond cake dusted with powdered sugar and marked with the cross of St. James, a sweet treat that is both symbolic and delicious.

5. Basque Country

Pintxos: Small snacks typically enjoyed with a drink, similar to tapas. They include a variety of toppings such as seafood, meats, and vegetables on a slice of bread.

Txangurro: Spider crab prepared with a rich sauce, reflecting the region's seafood heritage.

Bacalao a la Vizcaína: Salt cod in a tomato and red pepper sauce, showcasing the Basque love for seafood.

6. Asturias

Fabada Asturiana: A hearty bean stew made with white beans, chorizo, morcilla, and pork. Perfect for refueling after a long day of walking.

Sidra: Traditional Asturian cider, poured from a height to aerate it. Enjoy it in local cider houses.

Cachopo: Breaded and fried beef fillets stuffed with ham and cheese, a substantial and satisfying dish.

7. Cantabria

Sobao Pasiego: A rich, buttery sponge cake, ideal for breakfast or a snack.

Quesada Pasiega: A traditional cheesecake made with fresh cow's milk, sugar, butter, and eggs.

Rabas: Fried calamari, often served as a tapa or appetizer.

Tips for Enjoying Regional Cuisine

1. Try Local Specialties: Each region has its own unique dishes that are not to be missed. Don't hesitate to ask locals for their recommendations.

2. Visit Local Markets: Exploring local markets is a great way to discover fresh, regional ingredients and sample a variety of foods.

3. Join a Cooking Class: Many regions offer cooking classes where you can learn to prepare traditional dishes. It's a fun way to immerse yourself in the local culture.

4. Pair with Local Wines: Spain is renowned for its wines. Each region along the Camino has its own specialties, from the robust reds of La Rioja to the crisp whites of Galicia.

5. Enjoy Tapas and Pintxos: These small, shareable dishes allow you to sample a wide range of flavors and ingredients. They're perfect for a light meal or snack.

6. Embrace Seasonal Foods: Many regional dishes feature seasonal ingredients. Eating what's in season ensures you get the freshest and most flavorful foods.

Personal Experiences

1. Authentic Flavors: Sampling local dishes like Pulpo a la Gallega and Fabada Asturiana gave me a deeper appreciation for the region's culinary traditions. The flavors were both comforting and exciting.

2. Culinary Conversations: Sharing meals with fellow pilgrims often led to fascinating conversations about food and culture. It was a great way to connect and learn from each other.

3. Memorable Meals: Some of my most memorable moments on the Camino involved food, from a hearty stew in a small village to enjoying pintxos in a bustling bar. These experiences added richness to my journey.

Exploring regional cuisine is a delicious and integral part of the Camino de Santiago. Each meal offers an opportunity to connect with the local culture and savor the diverse flavors of Spain. Whether you're enjoying a simple tapa or a hearty stew, these culinary delights will fuel your journey and create lasting memories.

Art and Architecture of the Camino

The Camino de Santiago is not only a spiritual and physical journey but also an exploration of the rich artistic and architectural heritage of Spain. As you walk along the various routes, you will encounter stunning examples of Romanesque, Gothic, Renaissance, and Baroque art and architecture. Here are some of the key artistic and architectural highlights you can expect to see along the Camino:

1. Romanesque Architecture

Simplicity and Solidity: Characterized by thick walls, round arches, and sturdy pillars, Romanesque architecture evokes a sense of solidity and timelessness.

Notable Examples:

Church of San Martín in Frómista: This 11th-century church is a perfect example of Romanesque architecture with its symmetrical design and beautifully carved capitals.

Santiago de Compostela Cathedral (Original Romanesque Elements): While the cathedral has undergone various modifications, its original Romanesque core, including the Portico of Glory, is a masterpiece of medieval art.

2. Gothic Architecture

Height and Light: Gothic architecture is known for its verticality, pointed arches, ribbed vaults, and large stained glass windows that fill the interiors with light.

Notable Examples:

León Cathedral: Known as the "Pulchra Leonina," this cathedral is famous for its magnificent stained glass windows, which are among the finest in Europe.

Burgos Cathedral: A UNESCO World Heritage site, this Gothic cathedral features intricate facades, stunning spires, and an impressive interior filled with artistic treasures.

3. Renaissance and Plateresque Architecture

Elegance and Detail: Renaissance architecture brought a renewed focus on symmetry, proportion, and the use of classical elements. The Plateresque style, unique to Spain, is characterized by its ornate and intricate decoration.

Notable Examples:

Hospital de San Marcos in León: Originally a pilgrim hospital, this building is a stunning example of Spanish Renaissance architecture with its richly decorated façade.

University of Salamanca: The Plateresque façade of the university is a masterpiece of detailed stonework, featuring intricate carvings and decorations.

4. Baroque Architecture

Drama and Grandeur: Baroque architecture is known for its dynamic shapes, extravagant details, and a sense of movement and grandeur.

Notable Examples:

Santiago de Compostela Cathedral (Baroque Façade): The western façade, known as the Obradoiro, is a splendid example of Baroque architecture, adding a dramatic and ornate entrance to the pilgrimage's final destination.

Convent of San Esteban in Salamanca: This convent features an elaborate Baroque façade and a richly decorated interior.

5. Mudejar Architecture

Fusion of Cultures: Mudejar architecture is a unique blend of Christian and Islamic artistic traditions, characterized by the use of brick, tilework, and intricate geometric patterns.

Notable Examples:

San Tirso Church in Sahagún: This church features a mix of Romanesque and Mudejar styles, with distinctive brickwork and decorative arches.

San Lorenzo de Sahagún: Another fine example of Mudejar architecture with its distinctive use of brick and decorative motifs.

Artistic Highlights Along the Camino

1. Portico of Glory (Santiago de Compostela Cathedral):

Masterpiece of Medieval Sculpture: Created by Master Mateo in the 12th century, the Portico of Glory is an extraordinary example of Romanesque sculpture, depicting scenes from the Last Judgment with remarkable detail and expressiveness.

2. Altarpieces:

Intricate and Ornate: Many churches along the Camino feature stunning altarpieces (retablos) that are richly decorated with carvings, paintings, and gold leaf. Notable examples include the altarpiece in the Burgos Cathedral and the retablo in the Monastery of San Juan de Ortega.

3. Stained Glass Windows:

Vibrant Colors and Light: Gothic cathedrals like those in León and Burgos are renowned for their magnificent stained glass windows, which fill the interiors with vibrant colors and light, depicting biblical scenes and saints.

4. Frescoes and Mural Paintings:

Historical Narratives: Frescoes and murals adorn many churches and chapels along the Camino, offering glimpses into the religious and cultural history of the region. The murals in the Church of Santa María in Uncastillo and the frescoes in the Church of San Pedro de la Nave are notable examples.

Tips for Appreciating Art and Architecture on the Camino

1. Take Your Time:

Savor the Details: Spend time exploring the architectural details and artworks in the churches, cathedrals, and historical buildings you visit. Appreciate the craftsmanship and artistry that went into their creation.

2. Join Guided Tours:

Gain Insights: Many sites offer guided tours that provide valuable insights into the history, architecture, and art. These tours can enhance your understanding and appreciation of what you see.

3. Visit Museums:

Explore Further: Museums along the Camino, such as the Museo de la Catedral in Santiago de Compostela and the Museo de Burgos, house important collections of religious art and artifacts that offer deeper insights into the region's artistic heritage.

4. Document Your Journey:

Capture Memories: Take photographs and keep a journal of the art and architecture you encounter.

Documenting your observations and reflections can enrich your pilgrimage experience.

5. Engage with Locals:

Learn from Residents: Local residents and parishioners can offer fascinating stories and perspectives about the art and architecture in their communities. Engaging with them can provide a more personal connection to the sites you visit.

Experiencing the art and architecture along the Camino de Santiago is a journey through time, showcasing the rich cultural heritage and artistic achievements of Spain. Each church, cathedral, and historical site tells a story, inviting you to explore and appreciate the beauty and history that enriches your pilgrimage.

Chapter 9

Completing the Journey

Reaching Santiago de Compostela

After weeks or even months of walking, the sight of Santiago de Compostela marks the culmination of your incredible journey along the Camino de Santiago. Reaching this historic city is an emotional and triumphant moment for every pilgrim. Here's what you can expect and how to make the most of your arrival in Santiago de Compostela:

Arrival in Santiago

1. Emotional Arrival:

Feelings of Achievement: As you approach Santiago, you'll likely experience a mix of emotions—joy, relief, and a profound sense of accomplishment.

First Glimpse of the Cathedral: The sight of the spires of the Cathedral of Santiago de Compostela is a moment of awe and reverence for many pilgrims.

2. Entering the City:

Pilgrim's Mass: Attend the Pilgrim's Mass at the cathedral, which takes place daily at noon. This special mass includes the swinging of the Botafumeiro, a large incense burner, on certain days.

Plaza del Obradoiro: The main square in front of the cathedral is where pilgrims gather to celebrate and reflect on their journey. It's a place filled with emotions and stories.

The Cathedral of Santiago de Compostela

1. Historical Significance:

Tomb of Saint James: The cathedral is believed to house the remains of Saint James the Apostle, making it a major pilgrimage site since the Middle Ages.

Architectural Marvel: The cathedral is a stunning example of Romanesque, Gothic, and Baroque architecture.

2. Pilgrim Rituals:

Embrace the Saint: It is customary to hug the statue of Saint James behind the main altar, a gesture of gratitude and reverence.

Visit the Crypt: Pay your respects at the tomb of Saint James in the crypt beneath the main altar.

Pilgrim's Office: Visit the Pilgrim's Office to receive your Compostela certificate. Ensure your Pilgrim Passport (Credencial) is stamped at least twice a day in the last 100 kilometers (if walking) or 200 kilometers (if cycling).

Exploring Santiago de Compostela

1. Historical Sites:

Monastery of San Martín Pinario: A stunning monastery located near the cathedral, offering insight into the region's religious history.

Museo del Pueblo Gallego: This museum showcases the cultural heritage of Galicia, including traditional crafts, costumes, and architecture.

2. Culinary Delights:

Seafood: Galicia is famous for its seafood. Enjoy dishes like Pulpo a la Gallega (Galician-style octopus) and fresh shellfish.

Tarta de Santiago: A traditional almond cake, often enjoyed with a cup of coffee or a glass of local wine.

Local Markets: Visit Mercado de Abastos to explore local produce, cheeses, meats, and other regional specialties.

3. Cultural Activities:

Galician Music and Dance: Experience traditional Galician music and dance at local bars and cultural centers.

Street Performers: The streets of Santiago are alive with musicians, artists, and performers, adding to the vibrant atmosphere.

Reflecting on Your Journey

1. Personal Reflection:

Journal Writing: Take time to write about your experiences, thoughts, and feelings in a journal. Reflecting on your journey can provide closure and a deeper understanding of your pilgrimage.

Gratitude: Reflect on the people you met, the challenges you overcame, and the lessons you learned. Express gratitude for the journey and the growth it brought.

2. Connecting with Other Pilgrims:

Share Stories: Gather with fellow pilgrims to share stories and experiences. These conversations can be both healing and celebratory.

Exchange Contact Information: Keep in touch with the friends you made along the way. Many lifelong friendships are formed on the Camino.

Continuing the Journey

1. Finisterre and Muxía:

Extended Pilgrimage: Some pilgrims choose to continue their journey to Finisterre (Fisterra) and Muxía on the Atlantic coast. Finisterre is known as the "end of the world," and reaching it is a powerful symbol of completion.

Burning of Clothes: At Finisterre, some pilgrims partake in the tradition of burning a piece of clothing or their boots as a symbol of renewal and new beginnings.

2. Return Home:

Integration: Integrate the lessons and insights gained from the Camino into your daily life. The journey doesn't end in Santiago; it continues as you return home with a renewed perspective.

3. Future Pilgrimages:

Explore Other Routes: Consider walking other Camino routes or different pilgrimage paths around the world. Each route offers unique experiences and insights.

Tips for Making the Most of Your Arrival

1. Plan Ahead: Make reservations for accommodation in Santiago well in advance, especially during peak pilgrimage seasons.

2.Take Your Time: Allow yourself several days in Santiago to fully experience the city and its offerings.

3. Celebrate: Treat yourself to a special meal or activity to celebrate your accomplishment.

Reaching Santiago de Compostela is a profound and transformative experience. It marks the culmination of your physical journey but also the beginning of a deeper spiritual and personal reflection. Embrace the emotions, the history, and the community that you find in Santiago, and let it enrich your Camino experience.

The Pilgrim's Mass and Rituals

Reaching Santiago de Compostela is an emotional and spiritual milestone for every pilgrim. One of the most significant aspects of this achievement is participating in the Pilgrim's Mass at the Cathedral of Santiago de Compostela. This mass, along with other rituals, offers a profound sense of closure and celebration. Here's what you need to know about the Pilgrim's Mass and the associated rituals:

The Pilgrim's Mass

1. Daily Service:

Time: The Pilgrim's Mass is held daily at noon. During peak pilgrimage seasons, additional masses may be offered.

Location: The mass takes place in the Cathedral of Santiago de Compostela, a stunning architectural masterpiece that serves as the final destination for pilgrims.

2. Significance:

Spiritual Reflection: The Pilgrim's Mass is a time for reflection, gratitude, and spiritual connection. It offers pilgrims an opportunity to give thanks for their journey and to celebrate their accomplishment.

Community Gathering: Attending the mass with fellow pilgrims from around the world fosters a sense of community and shared purpose.

3. The Botafumeiro:

Giant Thurible: One of the highlights of the Pilgrim's Mass is the swinging of the Botafumeiro, a giant incense burner. This tradition dates back to the Middle Ages and was originally used to fumigate the cathedral.

Spectacle: The Botafumeiro, which weighs about 80 kg (176 lbs) and is 1.5 meters (4.9 feet) tall, swings from the cathedral's ceiling in a grand arc, filling the air with incense. This ceremony is typically performed on special occasions and certain holy days.

Pilgrim Rituals at the Cathedral

1. Hugging the Saint:

Statue of Saint James: Behind the main altar is a statue of Saint James (Santiago). It is a tradition for pilgrims to hug the statue as a gesture of reverence and gratitude.

Personal Reflection: This ritual allows pilgrims to have a personal moment with the saint, reflecting on their journey and the challenges they have overcome.

2. Visiting the Crypt:

Tomb of Saint James: Beneath the main altar is the crypt where the relics of Saint James are believed to be housed. Pilgrims can visit the crypt to pay their respects and offer prayers.

Historical Significance: This visit is a poignant reminder of the historical and spiritual significance of the Camino de Santiago.

3. Receiving the Compostela:

Pilgrim's Office: To receive the Compostela, the official certificate of completion, visit the Pilgrim's Office located near the cathedral. Ensure your Pilgrim Passport (Credencial) is stamped at least twice a day in the last 100 kilometers (if walking) or 200 kilometers (if cycling).

Certificate: The Compostela is a beautiful document written in Latin that acknowledges your achievement. For those who completed the Camino for non-religious reasons, a Certificate of Welcome is available.

Additional Rituals and Activities

1. Attending Other Services:

Vespers and Confession: The cathedral offers Vespers (evening prayers) and confession services. Participating in these can enhance your spiritual experience and provide additional moments of reflection.

2. Lighting a Candle:

Symbol of Prayer: Lighting a candle in the cathedral is a traditional act of prayer and remembrance. Many pilgrims light candles in gratitude or in memory of loved ones.

3. Exploring the Cathedral:

Cathedral Museum: Visit the museum to learn more about the history and art of the cathedral. It houses a vast collection of religious artifacts, sculptures, and tapestries.

Portico of Glory: Admire the Portico of Glory, a masterpiece of Romanesque sculpture located at the cathedral's entrance.

Tips for Participating in the Pilgrim's Mass and Rituals

1. Arrive Early: The cathedral can get crowded, especially during peak seasons. Arrive early to secure a good seat and to have some quiet time for personal reflection.

2. Respect the Space: The cathedral is a sacred space. Maintain a respectful demeanor, dress modestly, and follow any guidelines provided by the staff.

3. Be Present: Fully immerse yourself in the experience. Whether it's attending the mass, hugging the statue of

Saint James, or visiting the crypt, be present in the moment and allow yourself to feel the emotions of your journey.

Personal Experiences

1. A Sense of Closure: Participating in the Pilgrim's Mass provided a profound sense of closure to my journey. The mass was a time to reflect on the miles walked, the friendships made, and the personal growth achieved.

2. Community and Connection: Sharing this experience with fellow pilgrims from around the world created a deep sense of connection and community. It was heartwarming to see the diversity of people united by a common goal.

3. Spiritual Renewal: The rituals and the atmosphere of the cathedral fostered a sense of spiritual renewal. It was a time to offer gratitude, seek blessings, and find peace.

The Pilgrim's Mass and associated rituals at the Cathedral of Santiago de Compostela are central to the Camino experience. They offer moments of reflection, celebration, and spiritual connection, marking the culmination of your pilgrimage in a deeply meaningful way. Embrace these traditions as a way to honor your journey and the countless pilgrims who have walked this path before you.

Continuing to Finisterre and Muxía

While Santiago de Compostela is the traditional end point of the Camino de Santiago, many pilgrims choose to extend their journey to Finisterre (Fisterra) and Muxía on the rugged coast of Galicia. This continuation is often seen as a way to bring further closure and reflection to the pilgrimage. Here's what you need to know about extending your journey to these beautiful coastal towns:

The Route to Finisterre and Muxía

1. Overview:

Distance: The journey from Santiago to Finisterre is approximately 90 kilometers (56 miles), and from Finisterre to Muxía, it's about 29 kilometers (18 miles). The route can be completed in about 3-5 days, depending on your pace.

Terrain: The terrain varies from forest paths to coastal trails, offering stunning views and a peaceful walking experience.

2. Stages:

Day 1: Santiago to Negreira (21 km/13 miles): This first stage takes you through small villages and beautiful countryside. Negreira is a quaint town where you can find accommodation and services.

Day 2: Negreira to Olveiroa (33 km/20 miles): This longer stage includes a mix of forest trails and rural landscapes. Olveiroa is a small village with pilgrim accommodations.

Day 3: Olveiroa to Cee (18 km/11 miles): The route continues through scenic landscapes, with the first glimpses of the Atlantic Ocean as you approach Cee.

Day 4: Cee to Finisterre (12 km/7.5 miles): A shorter stage that follows the coastline, leading you to the historic town of Finisterre.

For those continuing to Muxía:

Day 5: Finisterre to Muxía (29 km/18 miles): This stage takes you along coastal paths to the serene town of Muxía.

Highlights of Finisterre

1. Cape Finisterre:

End of the World: Historically known as the "end of the world," Cape Finisterre is a place of great significance and symbolism for pilgrims.

Lighthouse: The iconic lighthouse at Cape Finisterre is a popular spot for reflection and photos. It's a tradition for some pilgrims to watch the sunset here.

2. Rituals:

Burning of Clothes or Boots: Some pilgrims burn a piece of clothing or their boots as a symbol of renewal and new beginnings. This ritual is often done at the designated fire pit near the lighthouse.

Collection of the Final Credential Stamp: At the Finisterre Pilgrim Office, you can collect the final stamp for your Pilgrim Passport and receive the "Finisterrana" certificate.

3. Beaches:

Langosteira Beach: A beautiful beach near Finisterre, perfect for a refreshing swim or a relaxing stroll after your long journey.

Highlights of Muxía

1. Sanctuary of Our Lady of the Boat (Santuario da Virxe da Barca):

Legend and Spirituality: This sanctuary is linked to the legend of the Virgin Mary arriving in a stone boat to encourage Saint James. The site offers a peaceful and spiritual atmosphere.

Pedra de Abalar: The famous "balancing rock" near the sanctuary is believed to have miraculous properties.

2. Coastal Beauty:

Stunning Views: The coastal paths to Muxía offer breathtaking views of the Atlantic Ocean and the rugged Galician coastline.

Relaxation: Muxía is a serene town where you can relax and reflect on your journey, away from the hustle and bustle of Santiago.

Practical Tips

1. Accommodation:

Book Ahead: While the route is less crowded than the Camino Francés, it's still wise to book accommodations in advance, especially during peak season.

Pilgrim Hostels and Albergues: There are numerous pilgrim hostels and albergues along the route offering affordable lodging.

2. Supplies and Services:

Food and Water: Carry sufficient water and snacks, as there are some stretches with limited services.

Local Information: Check local information centers for updates on the route and recommendations for places to stay and eat.

3. Physical Preparation:

Rest and Recovery: Ensure you're physically ready to continue walking after reaching Santiago. Take a rest day if needed before starting this next leg of the journey.

Foot Care: Continue to take good care of your feet, as the additional distance can be challenging after already completing the Camino.

Personal Reflections

1. Extended Reflection: Continuing to Finisterre and Muxía allowed me to extend the time of reflection and transition. The additional days of walking provided more opportunities for introspection and appreciating the journey.

2. Natural Beauty: The coastal scenery and peaceful paths offered a different kind of beauty compared to the rest of the Camino. Watching the sunset at Finisterre was a particularly memorable and symbolic moment.

3. Deeper Connections: Meeting fellow pilgrims who also chose to continue to Finisterre and Muxía created deeper connections and shared experiences.

Extending your pilgrimage to Finisterre and Muxía can be a deeply rewarding experience, offering further reflection, stunning natural beauty, and a sense of ultimate completion. Whether you choose to continue your journey or not, embracing the spirit of the Camino and carrying its lessons forward into your life is the true culmination of this remarkable journey.

Reflections and Life After the Camino

Walking the Camino de Santiago is more than a physical journey; it is a transformative experience that often leads to profound personal insights and growth. As you complete your pilgrimage and return to everyday life, the lessons and reflections from the Camino can continue to influence and enrich your life. Here's how you can reflect on your journey and integrate its lessons into your daily life:

Reflecting on Your Journey

1. Personal Insights:

Journaling: Take time to journal about your experiences, challenges, and the personal growth you've experienced. Writing helps solidify your reflections and serves as a keepsake of your journey.

Meditation and Quiet Time: Spend quiet time reflecting on what you've learned about yourself, your values, and your goals. Meditation can help deepen these reflections.

2. Gratitude:

Thankfulness: Reflect on the people you met, the hospitality you received, and the beauty you experienced. Practicing gratitude can enhance your sense of fulfillment.

Letters of Thanks: Consider writing letters to individuals or communities that made a significant impact on your journey. This can be a meaningful way to express your appreciation.

3. Lessons Learned:

Challenges Overcome: Identify the challenges you faced and overcame. Reflect on the resilience and resourcefulness you discovered within yourself.

Spiritual Growth: Consider the spiritual insights and growth you experienced. Reflect on how these can guide your future decisions and actions.

Integrating Lessons into Daily Life

1. Simplifying Life:

Declutter: The Camino teaches the value of simplicity. Consider decluttering your living space and focusing on what truly matters.

Mindful Consumption: Adopt mindful consumption habits, prioritizing quality over quantity and reducing unnecessary purchases.

2. Maintaining Physical Activity:

Regular Exercise: Incorporate regular physical activity into your routine. Walking, hiking, or other forms of exercise can help maintain the physical benefits you gained on the Camino.

Outdoor Adventures: Continue exploring nature through outdoor activities. Spending time in nature can help you stay connected to the sense of peace you found on the Camino.

3. Continuing Spiritual Practices:

Daily Reflection: Set aside time each day for reflection, meditation, or prayer. This practice can help maintain the spiritual insights you gained.

Community Involvement: Engage with your local community or a spiritual group. Sharing your experiences and supporting others can deepen your sense of connection and purpose.

4. Cultivating Gratitude and Mindfulness:

Gratitude Journal: Keep a gratitude journal to regularly note what you're thankful for. This practice can help maintain a positive outlook.

Mindful Living: Practice mindfulness in daily activities, staying present and fully engaged in each moment.

Sharing Your Experience

1. Storytelling:

Share Your Story: Share your Camino experience with friends, family, and community groups. Your story can inspire and encourage others.

Public Speaking: Consider giving talks or presentations about your journey. Public libraries, schools, and community centers may welcome your insights.

2. Supporting Future Pilgrims:

Offer Advice: Join online forums or local Camino groups to offer advice and support to future pilgrims.

Volunteer: Consider volunteering at pilgrim hostels or organizations that support the Camino. Your experience can provide valuable insights and encouragement to others.

3. Creative Expression:

Art and Photography: Use art, photography, or other creative outlets to express and share your journey.

Writing: Write articles, blog posts, or even a book about your Camino experience. Sharing your reflections can be therapeutic and inspiring.

Planning Future Adventures

1. New Pilgrimages:

Explore Other Routes: Consider walking other Camino routes or different pilgrimage paths around the world. Each route offers unique experiences and insights.

Adventure Travel: Plan other adventure travel experiences that challenge and inspire you. The skills and resilience you gained on the Camino will serve you well.

2. Lifelong Learning:

Continued Growth: Embrace opportunities for lifelong learning. Attend workshops, courses, or retreats that align with the interests and insights you discovered on the Camino.

Cultural Exploration: Continue exploring different cultures and traditions. Travel with an open mind and heart, seeking to understand and connect with others.

Personal Reflections

1. Ongoing Transformation:

Embrace Change: Understand that the Camino is just the beginning of an ongoing journey of personal transformation. Be open to change and growth as you continue to integrate its lessons into your life.

Inner Peace: Strive to maintain the inner peace and clarity you found on the Camino. Regular reflection and mindfulness practices can help sustain this state of being.

2. Community and Connection:

Stay Connected: Maintain connections with fellow pilgrims and others you met along the way. These relationships can provide support and camaraderie.

Give Back: Find ways to give back to your community and support others on their journeys. Acts of kindness and service can deepen your sense of fulfillment and purpose.

Chapter 10

Insider Tips and Resources

Stories and Insights from Experienced Pilgrims

One of the most valuable aspects of preparing for the Camino de Santiago is learning from those who have walked the path before you. Experienced pilgrims offer a wealth of practical tips, heartfelt stories, and insightful reflections that can enrich your own journey. Here are some stories and insights from seasoned Camino walkers that will provide inspiration and guidance as you embark on your pilgrimage.

Stories from the Camino

1. Maria's Journey of Healing : Maria, a nurse from Italy, embarked on the Camino after a difficult period in her life. She shares: "I started the Camino to heal from a recent loss. Walking each day, I found solace in the rhythm of my steps and the kindness of strangers. One memorable moment was meeting an elderly man who had walked the Camino multiple times. His wisdom and warmth were a beacon of hope for me. By the time I reached Santiago, I felt a sense of peace and acceptance I hadn't felt in years."

2. Tom's Tale of Friendship : Tom, a software engineer from the United States, set out on the Camino to challenge himself physically. He recounts: "I expected a solo adventure, but what I found was a community. I met Jake, a fellow pilgrim from Australia, on my third day. We walked together, sharing stories and laughter. One night, in a small albergue, we joined a communal dinner where everyone shared their food and experiences. These moments of connection became the highlight of my journey. Jake and I are still in touch, planning our next adventure together."

3. Ana's Cultural Discovery : Ana, a history teacher from Spain, walked the Camino to explore her country's heritage. She explains: "Walking the Camino was like stepping back in time. I was fascinated by the historical sites, from ancient Roman bridges to medieval churches. In Castrojeriz, I stumbled upon a local festival celebrating Saint James, complete with traditional music and dance. These cultural experiences deepened my appreciation for my heritage and the timeless nature of the Camino."

Practical Tips from Experienced Pilgrims

1. Packing Essentials

Light and Efficient: "Pack light. You'll thank yourself later. Focus on essentials: good hiking boots, moisture-wicking socks, a quality backpack, and versatile clothing. Less is more." – John, UK

Multipurpose Items: "Bring multipurpose items like a sarong, which can serve as a towel, blanket, or sunshade." – Lisa, Canada

2. Health and Well-being

Foot Care: "Take care of your feet. Stop and treat hot spots immediately to prevent blisters. A small tube of Vaseline and some moleskin can be lifesavers." – Carlos, Spain

Hydration and Nutrition: "Stay hydrated and eat well. Carry a refillable water bottle and healthy snacks like nuts and dried fruit." – Emily, Australia

3. Navigating the Camino

Flexibility: "Have a plan, but stay flexible. Weather, health, or unexpected detours can change your itinerary. Embrace the unpredictability." – Marco, Italy

Local Knowledge: "Talk to locals and fellow pilgrims. They can provide the best advice on where to stay, eat, and find hidden gems." – Sophie, France

4. Accommodation Tips

Early Arrival: "Arrive early at albergues, especially in popular towns, to secure a bed. Some fill up quickly during peak season." – Ben, Germany

Variety: "Mix up your accommodations. Stay in albergues, hotels, and even monasteries to experience different aspects of the Camino." – Laura, USA

Emotional and Spiritual Insights

1. Embracing the Journey

Letting Go: "The Camino teaches you to let go—of schedules, of control, of expectations. Embrace each day as it comes and be open to the journey." – Paolo, Brazil

Presence: "Stay present. The Camino is as much about the inner journey as the physical one. Reflect on your thoughts and feelings each day." – Hana, Japan

2. Building Connections

Shared Experiences: "The bonds you form with fellow pilgrims are unique. Sharing the ups and downs of the journey creates deep connections that often last beyond the Camino." – David, South Africa

Kindness and Generosity: "Acts of kindness, whether receiving or giving, are the heart of the Camino. These moments remind you of the goodness in people." – Elena, Portugal

3. Post-Camino Integration

Continued Reflection: "Keep reflecting on your Camino experience once you return home. The lessons you learned and the clarity you gained can guide you in everyday life." – Isabel, Argentina

Staying Connected: "Stay connected with the Camino community. Whether through online groups or reunions, these connections can continue to support and inspire you." – Michael, USA

Resources for Pilgrims

1. Online Communities

Forums and Social Media: Join online forums and social media groups dedicated to the Camino de Santiago. These platforms are great for advice, support, and sharing experiences.

2. Books and Guides

Guidebooks: Invest in a good guidebook specific to the route you are walking.

Inspirational Reads: A Book like *To the Field of Stars* by Kevin A. Codd offer inspirational insights into the Camino experience.

3. Apps and Digital Resources

Navigation Apps: Use apps like Maps.me or Camino apps that provide detailed maps, route information, and accommodation listings.

Language Tools: Download language translation apps to help with communication, especially in rural areas where English may not be widely spoken.

Recommended Films and documentaries

Engaging with films about the Camino de Santiago can offer valuable insights and inspiration for your journey. These films provide a mix of personal stories, dramatic adaptations, and documentaries that capture the spirit, challenges, and rewards of the pilgrimage. Here are some highly recommended films to watch as you prepare for your Camino adventure:

1. The Way (2010)

Director: Emilio Estevez

Starring: Martin Sheen, Emilio Estevez

Overview: This heartfelt film follows Tom, an American doctor who travels to France to retrieve the body of his estranged son who died while walking the Camino. Tom decides to complete the journey in his son's honor, meeting other pilgrims and finding a renewed sense of purpose along the way.

Why Watch It?: "The Way" beautifully captures the transformative power of the Camino, highlighting themes of grief, healing, and community. Martin Sheen's performance adds depth and authenticity to the story.

2. Walking the Camino: Six Ways to Santiago (2013)

Director: Lydia B. Smith

Overview: This documentary follows six pilgrims from different backgrounds as they walk the Camino de Santiago. The film captures their challenges, triumphs, and personal transformations throughout the journey.

Why Watch It?: The documentary provides an authentic and intimate look at the pilgrimage, offering inspiration and practical insights from real pilgrims' experiences.

3. I'll Push You (2017)

Directors: Chris Karcher, Terry Parish

Overview: This documentary tells the inspiring story of two best friends, Justin Skeesuck and Patrick Gray. Justin, who uses a wheelchair due to a progressive neuromuscular disease, and Patrick embark on the Camino together, demonstrating the power of friendship and perseverance.

Why Watch It?: "I'll Push You" showcases the incredible strength of human spirit and the importance of companionship on the Camino, making it a deeply moving and uplifting film.

4. Footprints: The Path of Your Life (2016)

Director: Juan Manuel Cotelo

Overview: This documentary follows a group of American men led by a Catholic priest as they embark on the Camino de Santiago. Each pilgrim faces personal challenges and seeks spiritual growth throughout the journey.

Why Watch It?: The film provides a touching exploration of faith, brotherhood, and personal transformation, offering a unique perspective on the Camino experience.

5. The Way of St. James (Saint-Jacques... La Mecque) (2005)

Director: Coline Serreau

Overview: This French comedy-drama follows three estranged siblings who must walk the Camino together to receive their inheritance. Along the way, they confront their personal issues and reconnect with each other.

Why Watch It?: The film combines humor and drama, providing an entertaining yet insightful take on the Camino experience and the relationships formed along the way.

6. Camino Skies (2019)

Directors: Fergus Grady, Noel Smyth

Overview: This documentary follows six inspirational Australians and New Zealanders, each dealing with personal loss, as they set out on the Camino de Santiago. The film captures their emotional and physical journey, emphasizing the therapeutic aspects of the pilgrimage.

Why Watch It?: "Camino Skies" offers a powerful look at the resilience of the human spirit and the healing potential of the Camino, making it an inspiring watch for prospective pilgrims.

7. Strangers on the Earth (2016)

Director: Tristan Cook

Overview: This documentary focuses on the journey of Dane Johansen, an American cellist who walked the Camino with his cello, performing music in churches along the way. The film explores the experiences of various pilgrims and the profound impact of the journey.

Why Watch It?: The unique blend of music and pilgrimage offers a contemplative and artistic perspective on the Camino, highlighting the diverse motivations and experiences of pilgrims.

8. Pelerinages: The Road to Compostela (2004)

Director: Frederic Compain

Overview: This French documentary traces the history and significance of the Camino de Santiago, offering insights into the cultural and spiritual aspects of the pilgrimage.

Why Watch It?: The historical and cultural context provided by the documentary enriches the understanding of the Camino's importance and enduring appeal.

9. The Camino Voyage (2018)

Directors: Donal O'Ceilleachair

Overview: This documentary follows a group of Irish men as they embark on a traditional boat journey from Ireland to Santiago de Compostela, retracing the ancient pilgrimage route by sea.

Why Watch It?: The film highlights the spirit of adventure and the enduring nature of pilgrimage, offering a unique perspective on the Camino.

Watching films about the Camino de Santiago can provide valuable insights, inspiration, and a deeper understanding of the pilgrimage experience. These recommended films capture the essence of the Camino, from personal stories of transformation to the challenges and triumphs faced by pilgrims. As you prepare for your journey, these films can help you connect with the spirit of the Camino and offer a glimpse into the profound impact it has on those who walk its path.

Useful Apps and Websites

Leveraging technology can significantly enhance your Camino de Santiago experience, from planning your trip to navigating the route and staying connected with fellow pilgrims. Here are some of the most useful apps and websites to help you prepare for and enjoy your pilgrimage.

1. Camino de Santiago Apps

Camino Pilgrim – Wise Pilgrim Guides

Overview: This app offers detailed maps, route information, accommodation listings, and points of interest for various Camino routes.

Features: Offline maps, real-time updates, and user reviews of albergues and other accommodations.

Why Use It?: It's a comprehensive resource that covers multiple routes and provides essential information for your journey.

Buen Camino

Overview: Developed by the Xunta de Galicia, this app provides information on the main Camino routes, including the Camino Francés, Camino del Norte, and others.

Features: Interactive maps, accommodation details, services, and weather updates.

Why Use It?:It's an official app that offers reliable and up-to-date information directly from the regional authorities.

CaminoTool

Overview: This app offers practical information for pilgrims, including stages, distances, accommodations, and services along the route.

Features: Offline access, GPS tracking, and customizable itineraries.

Why Use It?: It's user-friendly and provides essential tools for planning and navigating your pilgrimage.

2. Navigation and Maps

Maps.me

Overview: An offline map app that provides detailed maps and navigation for any location worldwide.

Features: Downloadable maps, GPS navigation, and points of interest.

Why Use It?:It's incredibly useful for navigating rural areas with limited internet access.

Google Maps

Overview: A comprehensive mapping service with real-time navigation, traffic conditions, and local business information.

Features: Street view, public transportation routes, and offline maps.

Why Use It?:It's a versatile tool that can help you find your way around cities and towns along the Camino.

3. Language and Translation

Google Translate

Overview: A translation app that supports over 100 languages and offers text, voice, and image translation.

Features: Offline translation, conversation mode, and camera translation.

Why Use It?: It's invaluable for overcoming language barriers and communicating with locals.

Duolingo

Overview: A language-learning app that offers courses in multiple languages, including Spanish.

Features: Gamified lessons, progress tracking, and offline access.

Why Use it?: It's a fun and effective way to learn basic Spanish phrases and vocabulary before and during your trip.

4. Health and Fitness

Strava

Overview: A fitness tracking app that allows you to record and share your walking, running, or cycling activities.

Features: GPS tracking, performance analysis, and social sharing.

Why Use it?: It's great for tracking your daily progress and staying motivated.

MyFitnessPal

Overview: A nutrition and fitness tracking app that helps you monitor your diet and exercise.

Features: Food diary, calorie counter, and exercise log.

Why Use It?: It's useful for maintaining a balanced diet and staying healthy on the Camino.

5. Travel and Accommodation

Booking.com

Overview: A hotel and accommodation booking app that offers a wide range of lodging options.

Features: Reviews, maps, and booking management.

Why Use It? : It's helpful for finding and booking accommodations along the Camino.

Airbnb

Overview: An app for booking unique accommodations, including private rooms, homes, and experiences.

Features: Search filters, user reviews, and secure booking.

Why Use It?: It offers a variety of lodging options that can enhance your Camino experience.

Useful Websites

1. Camino de Santiago Resources

American Pilgrims on the Camino

Website: americanpilgrims.org

Overview: A comprehensive resource for American pilgrims, offering information on routes, packing lists, forums, and events.

Why Use It?: It's a supportive community with valuable resources and advice for pilgrims.

Camino de Santiago Forum

Website: caminodesantiago.me

Overview: An online forum where pilgrims can share experiences, ask questions, and offer advice.

Why use it?:It's a great place to connect with other pilgrims and get answers to specific questions.

Gronze

Website: gronze.com

Overview: A Spanish website that provides detailed route information, accommodation listings, and maps for the Camino de Santiago.

Why use it?: It's a highly detailed and reliable resource for planning your stages and finding accommodations.

2. Travel Planning

Rome2rio

Website: rome2rio.com

Overview: A travel planning website that shows how to get from one place to another by plane, train, bus, ferry, and car.

Why use it? :It's useful for planning your travel to and from the starting and ending points of your Camino.

Skyscanner

Website: skyscanner.com

Overview: A flight search engine that compares prices from different airlines and travel agencies.

Why use it? :It's great for finding affordable flights to Spain and other starting points on the Camino.

3. Health and Safety

Centers for Disease Control and Prevention (CDC)

Website: cdc.gov

Overview: Provides health information and travel advisories for international travelers.

Why use it?: It's important for staying informed about health recommendations and vaccination requirements.

World Health Organization (WHO)

Website: who.int

Overview: Offers global health information, including travel advisories and health guidelines.

Why use it ?: It's a reliable source for up-to-date health information and advice.

Staying Connected with the Camino Community

The Camino de Santiago is more than just a physical journey; it's a community of people bound by a shared experience. Staying connected with the Camino community after your pilgrimage can provide ongoing support, friendship, and inspiration. Here are some ways to stay connected with fellow pilgrims and continue to engage with the Camino spirit.

Online Communities and Forums

1. Camino de Santiago Forum

Website: Camino de Santiago Forum

Overview: An active online forum where pilgrims share experiences, ask questions, and provide advice.

Why Join: It's a great place to stay informed about Camino news, get travel tips, and connect with others who share your passion.

2. American Pilgrims on the Camino

Website: American Pilgrims on the Camino

Overview: A comprehensive resource for American pilgrims, offering information, forums, and local chapter events.

Why Join: The site offers a supportive community and opportunities to participate in events and gatherings across the United States.

3. Facebook Groups

Camino de Santiago (The Way of St. James)

Overview: A large and active Facebook group where members post photos, share stories, and offer advice.

Why Join: It's a convenient way to stay connected, share your experiences, and get inspired by others.

Camino Pilgrims

Overview: Another vibrant Facebook group focused on the Camino, where members discuss various routes and share helpful tips.

Why Join: It provides a diverse range of perspectives and experiences from pilgrims around the world.

Local Camino Groups and Associations

1. Local Chapters of American Pilgrims on the Camino

Overview: Various local chapters across the United States organize meetings, hikes, and events for past and future pilgrims.

Why Join: These local groups offer a way to meet fellow pilgrims in your area, participate in Camino-related activities, and share your experiences.

2. Confraternity of Saint James

Website: Confraternity of Saint James

Overview: A UK-based organization that supports pilgrims with information, events, and publications.

Why Join: It provides a wealth of resources and a strong community network for pilgrims in the UK.

3. Canadian Company of Pilgrims

Website: Canadian Company of Pilgrims

Overview: An organization that promotes the Camino and supports Canadian pilgrims through meetings, newsletters, and events.

Why Join: It offers a supportive community and useful resources for Canadian pilgrims.

Pilgrim Reunions and Events

1. Annual Gatherings

Overview: Many Camino organizations host annual gatherings and conferences where pilgrims can reconnect, share stories, and attend workshops.

Why Attend: These events are a wonderful opportunity to rekindle friendships, learn more about the Camino, and celebrate the pilgrimage community.

2. Local Meetups and Hikes

Overview: Local Camino groups often organize regular meetups and hikes, providing opportunities to stay active and connected.

Why Attend: Participating in these activities helps maintain the physical and social aspects of the Camino experience.

Volunteering and Giving Back

1. Volunteering at Albergues

Overview: Many former pilgrims return to volunteer at albergues along the Camino, helping to support new pilgrims on their journey.

Why Volunteer: It's a meaningful way to give back to the Camino community and stay connected with the pilgrimage spirit.

2. Supporting Camino Organizations

Overview: Donate to or volunteer with organizations that support the Camino, such as the American Pilgrims on the Camino, Confraternity of Saint James, and others.

Why Support: Your contributions help maintain the infrastructure and services that make the Camino accessible to future pilgrims.

Sharing Your Story

1. Blogging and Social Media

Overview: Share your Camino journey through a personal blog, Instagram, or other social media platforms.

Why Share: Your story can inspire and inform others considering the pilgrimage, and it helps you stay engaged with the Camino community.

2. Public Speaking and Presentations

Overview: Offer to speak about your Camino experience at local community centers, schools, or Camino organization events.

Why Speak: Sharing your story in person can deeply impact others and keep the Camino spirit alive in your community.

Continuing Your Pilgrimage

1. Walking Other Routes

Overview: Explore other Camino routes or different pilgrimage paths around the world.

Why Continue: Each route offers unique experiences and challenges, allowing you to continue your personal and spiritual journey.

2. Hosting Pilgrims

Overview: Offer hospitality to pilgrims passing through your area, providing a place to stay or sharing a meal.

Why Host: It's a way to extend the Camino's tradition of hospitality and meet fellow pilgrims from around the world.

Final Thoughts

Staying connected with the Camino community allows you to keep the spirit of the pilgrimage alive in your everyday life. Whether through online forums, local groups, volunteering, or sharing your story, these connections provide ongoing support, inspiration, and a sense of belonging. The Camino de Santiago is more than just a journey; it's a lifelong community that continues to grow and enrich your life long after you've reached Santiago de Compostela.

Printed in Great Britain
by Amazon